THE CORPORATION AND

putting it into practice

The Corporation and its Stakeholders: putting it into practice

GODFREY REHAAG

Copyright © Godfrey Rehaag, 2015

All rights reserved. No part of this book may be reproduced or retransmitted in any form or by any means without the prior written permission of the author.

Published by Godfrey Rehaag

www.rehaag.co.uk

Printed by CreateSpace, an Amazon.com company

ISBN: 1516887352
ISBN-13: 978-1516887354

THE CORPORATION AND ITS STAKEHOLDERS:

putting it into practice

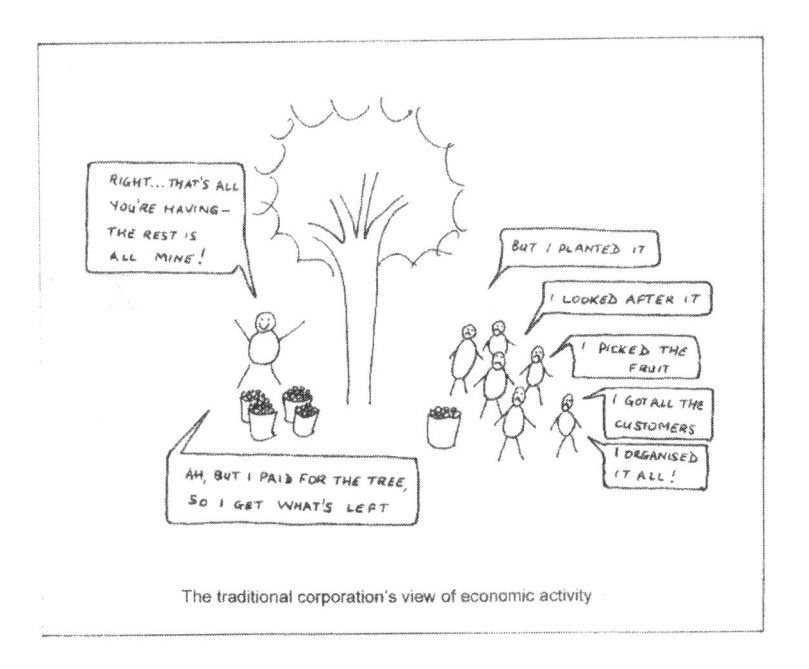

The traditional corporation's view of economic activity

Contents

Acknowledgements		9
Preface		11
1	What is business, and why do we do it?	14
2	The form a business takes: the corporation	26
3	A fresh look at the corporate model	36
4	Capital	54
5	The capital incentive problem	77
6	Corporate governance	89
7	Financial reporting	103
8	The contribution of labour	119
9	Thinking it through: some practical effects	124
10	Limited liability revisited	144
11	Equity units in practice: some details	164
12	The matter of taxation	172

13	Summary of the proposals for a new corporate model	190
14	Conclusions	206
References		213

Acknowledgements

In order to make this work more accessible to the lay reader, I have deliberately avoided the tendency to treat this book as scholarly or academic, and have accordingly not included footnotes or a bibliography, but some references have been unavoidable. I am indebted to *The Economist Newspaper Limited*, London, for a couple of relevant quotations, and to the other sources that are listed under 'references' at the end of this book. I also wish to record my appreciation of David Hatherly (Emeritus Professor of Accounting at the University of Edinburgh Business School), who is the only other person I have come across who has had similar insights to mine in relation to the existing corporate model; we both agree on what the problems are, but have explored different strategies to resolve them. Thanks go to various others for their support and encouragement, in particular Phil Jones (of the *Philosophical Discussion Group),* Brian Page (editor of *Mensa Magazine*) and the clients of my accountancy practice, who enabled me to pursue independent research. Finally I thank my wife Jane for her unwavering support and the provision of much peace and quiet!

Preface

For decades people have been pleading for the major corporations that dominate our business world to somehow reflect their responsibilities to a wider range of stakeholders than just their shareholders. This includes not just the workforce, but also suppliers (such as for supermarkets) and customers (such as for utility suppliers in monopoly situations). More recently, that call has extended to include an appeal to tackle the gross economic inequality that seems to be increasing across the nation, requiring corporations to somehow share out more fairly the rewards of their activities. Yet despite all that's been said by all sorts of people, frankly little has changed.

And a good thing, too, say the business and investor community – for they argue that this is because the existing corporation *works*. It delivers the goods, while the arguments of the activists are dismissed as 'worthy waffle' (to quote *The Economist*). But the business community is wrong too.

The problem is that each side in the debate only fights the ground on its own side, and as a result an unbridgeable gulf lies between them. There is no real comprehension of each other's arguments. The issue needs to be taken out of the realm of politics and sociology and into a more businesslike approach to creating wealth and rewarding effort. There's nothing *wrong* with business enterprise and economic activity – it's what generates the economic success that we all need. And yet at the same time it is patently absurd for the fruits of all our efforts to be gathered solely by those who possess capital, as that is one of the greatest sources of inequality and disharmony today.

High levels of taxation and regulation, or worker control, are one response: but if we *want* enterprise and economic activity – and it is difficult to see how we are going to get greater shares in economic success without them – then the answer cannot be to stifle business but to encourage it while reorganising it in a way that shares its benefits more equitably. There is only one way of reducing the curse of economic inequality while at the same time promoting the vitality of business activity, and that is to make the framework for enterprise – the structure of the corporation – fit for purpose in the twenty-first century.

The practical solution must therefore be to tackle what lies at the heart of capitalism: the form or model of the corporation. We need to restructure the corporate framework *without* capitalism. We need a practical, workable mechanism for including a wider range of stakeholders, thereby reducing economic inequality: and that is precisely what this book offers.

This book proposes a radical but businesslike solution: changing the framework of the corporation to make it work better for all those involved in it, by removing the dominance of capital as the sole source of enterprise and the owner of economic activity, and instead promoting the opportunity and incentive for all types of contribution to economic activity to participate in the corporation and share in the benefits it brings.

Despite incremental changes to the present corporate model since its introduction 170 years ago, the model remains unashamedly Victorian. Its proponents claim that it has enabled market economics to achieve the greatest ever leap in the prosperity of the West. In fact it could be argued that the western world's prosperity was as much the result of market economics, the rule of law, the existence of just and fair institutions, and the availability of private venture capital, as it was to the corporation. The corporation is undoubtedly failing, and failing in many directions – there is dismay at the disinterest of the shareholders, ineffective supervision of the directors, weaknesses in auditing and in corporate governance, the lack of recognition of the input and interests of a wider range of stakeholders, and short-termism resulting from an obsession about share price, quite apart from the ever-rising and unjust inequality. These problems are due to *structural* faults in the model. Proposals for reform are mostly incremental, and concentrate on adding to the burden of regulations rather than on thoroughly reconsidering the underlying structure itself – or else the various proposals are either wholly unfriendly to business, or too worthy and impractical.

So this book starts at the beginning, and asks how and why we humans do business in the first place. We abandon the existing presumption that all economic activity and enterprise is solely the result of idle spare wealth, with all other contributors to economic activity relegated to the role of economic servants. We question the whole function and purpose of the corporation, proposing a dynamic model of business entity that responds *organically* to changing circumstances. Instead of regulatory impositions upon the present model, we bring free market economics to the heart of corporate activity. We seek an elegant, integrated solution for which the dynamics are fully explored and argued to their conclusion: thereby devising an essentially *practical* model which should achieve automatically much of what the present model is acknowledged to lack.

Inevitably, with a subject as complex as the corporate structure, there is a lot of detail in this book: so if you simply want a good flavour of what the issues are about, please read Chapter 13 and the conclusions in Chapter 14.

The aim of this imaginative and provocative analysis, by someone steeped in the art of business, is to make business work better for everyone involved in it, as well as for the community as a whole.

1 What is business, and why do we do it?

Introduction
What this book aims to do is to cast aside all our existing presumptions about the way we humans do business with one another, and think entirely afresh about how we would organise the whole structure of economic activity if we could start all over again from square one, but with our present state of knowledge and civilised values. The result should be a proposal for a framework for business organisation that perfectly fits our human needs at the present time. We shall then explore all the implications of the new model and test it against the different stresses that it will have to deal with. Finally, we shall compare the proposed new model with the existing model of the corporation and see if we can demonstrate that it will indeed achieve a better outcome for everyone involved.

What is economic activity?
In the act of becoming civilised, mankind has become a social creature: we have become dependent upon each other. Every single one of us has to inter-relate with other human beings in order to satisfy even our most basic needs; if we don't, we soon become cavemen again. Why? Well, just imagine everyday life without social interaction. We would have to gather or grow all our own food and drink, gather firewood to keep us warm, find and process the material to make all our own clothes and shoes, work out how to make tools, and how to build our own homes; and throughout all this, we would have to defend ourselves against every imaginable external threat. 'Every man is enemy to every man... no arts; no letters; no society... and the life of man, solitary, poor, nasty, brutish, and short' (Hobbes 1651). Without interacting with others, we would never have the time, the resources or the security to think and

develop and progress. We can be self-sufficient, but not civilised at the same time. For purely practical reasons as much as for emotional preference, therefore, the modern human being cannot survive without interaction with his or her fellows. That, in simple terms, is the essential basis of our civilisation.

Probably the most elementary property belonging to all living organisms is *the drive to self-organise*. This is a fundamental property of life, matter and energy throughout the universe; and humankind has refined and adapted this natural drive, so that we have evolved to *want* to civilise. By this is meant that we want to join together into social groups so as to utilise and compensate for the different talents, strengths and weaknesses we each possess. In every corner of the human world, human beings group naturally together to share tasks – usually without even thinking about it – so that the needs of all are met while each person may actually be doing something individual for which he or she is best suited. This observation is something prosaically described by economists as 'division of labour'.

Division of labour can be seen to have been a fundamental feature of prehistoric human gatherings as long ago as 100,000 years, and possibly even longer, with the first use of tools and meat-eating by humans. It was formally acknowledged in writing as long ago as four centuries before Christ (by Plato in his *'Republic'*) that division of labour and the loss of man's self-sufficiency made a system of commercial organisation inevitable, and it is this commercial organisation that might loosely be called 'doing business'.

So this is what we have. Nature provides us with natural resources; mankind offers demand for those resources and, at the same time, but not always in a perfectly matching way, offers the ability to manage those natural resources so as to satisfy that demand. This then is what is the potential for 'economic activity' or doing business:

1. we have an abundance of natural resources, although never seemingly quite enough or in the right place or condition, so we need to make the most of them by putting in the necessary effort to maximise their overall value to mankind; and

2. we have the people to do this – people with a variety of abilities (also sometimes in short supply) and a variety of needs – but

with the general ability and drive to organise themselves at every level.

A need is, of course, not just a demand for 'products' or 'services'; it is also a need for occupation, achievement, satisfaction and self-fulfilment, and even help, support, companionship and love. That is the substance of economic activity, and when it works, it can be highly effective – it can achieve a large proportion of all our human needs, automatically. The very act of providing goods or services for others is one's own source of occupation and fulfilment. For this reason, economic activity is highly relevant to all of us, not just to business people.

So we need economic activity. But just *how* does this economic activity happen? We could suggest that some system or mechanism of economic organisation needs to be in place so as to provide the framework within which economic activity may occur between the various parties concerned. But that still doesn't explain how it actually happens, what the *motivation* is for 'doing it'. Economic activity exists not only because there is a greater demand than the scarce resources can satisfy: that may be the opportunity, but the *drive* behind economic activity often has a far broader motivation. In the more developed areas of today's world, it is more often the quest for occupation, achievement and satisfaction that drives people to produce or offer goods or services that then go seeking or creating demand. Indeed, it would be more proper to say that economic activity exists *because we are civilised human beings*: because, through division of labour, we each seek to do only that which we want to do, can do, or are best at doing. The inevitable consequence of this is that (a) exchanges have to be arranged between us, and (b) teamwork has to be arranged for larger ventures; but that still doesn't explain *how* it happens.

So let's think for a moment about the precise purpose we have in doing business. Economic activity would seem to operate at three different levels:

1   Its primary function must be to obtain, create, process, distribute and service the real resources necessary for human sustenance, comfort and satisfaction generally, i.e., to improve the lot of man by maximising the value to him of the natural resources available.

2   The secondary function which must follow, indeed is inseparable from this, is the system or structure for achieving the primary function, but presented in terms not of allocation of real resources (or satisfaction of needs) but of distribution of notional reward, i.e., a system of cash or monetary values to enable exchanges to take place between those participating in the activity concerned. In every business, cash comes in from sales and then goes out again to pay for purchases, wages, interest, rent, etc. To put it rather bluntly, in the developed world, the immediate purpose of business is not to allocate resources for physical survival, but to make a living, to make money. The urge to accumulate a store of treasure has been a potent driving force behind most of mankind since prehistory.

3   The third function – the least important in a primordial society, but of increasing importance as civilisation develops – is the matter of providing opportunity for occupation and self-fulfilment.

If we are to be more precise, and we need to be, we can really only describe level (1) as the *function* and levels (2) and (3) as *motives*. After all, the 'function' of reproduction may be to sustain a population, while the more immediate and pleasurable 'motive' is usually more selfish and individual – but the motive ensures the achievement of the same end result. This comparison illustrates how we need to take advantage of human nature by accepting and exploiting a less noble motive in order to achieve the proper ultimate function. The command economies, such as communism, concentrate solely upon achieving the critical function (1), and ignore the reality of the typically human motives (2) and (3). By contrast, to individual participants in the market economy, function (1) is left to follow naturally as the automatic result of the other two. But we are jumping the gun here: what we were asking was, *how exactly* do you make business happen?

How business happens
Essentially, there would seem to be only two broad approaches to the arrangement of economic activity:

1. One that leaves the people to sort it out among themselves, harnessing natural human drives: the complex but powerful dynamics which drive mankind can be taken into account and exploited in order to drive the framework.

2. One that's organised in some way – a prescriptive or 'command' economy: somebody works out what each person needs, and what each person can provide, and then sets out to plan and arrange all the necessary matching.

Examples of natural human drives are the impulses of consideration, fairness and justice, supported by some standard of morality. This works efficiently in the family setting and in the smaller community, especially when there is a clear common identity of purpose, such as in times of communal difficulty or individual tragedy, but it is perceived to be less effective in a larger or more complex setting, when selfish impulses intervene and there is less identity with others. It is these selfish impulses which are then turned to good effect in the market economy, where the natural motivation to acquire and retain personal economic wealth is utilised as the engine to make the system work. This motivation is of course not just simple greed for power and wealth, but also a search for individual security, achievement, self-respect, pride, fulfilment, and so on. It is well established that people find self-worth in a sense of purpose (such as the successful building up of a business, even if it is not particularly profitable), as well as through peer respect, often simply earned through employment 'position' as much as by possession of pure economic wealth resulting from that. Thus an apparently pure economic motivation is not necessarily to be disparaged. It is necessary, of course, to recognise that the economic motivation, while powerful, is not the only one to drive the human being; indeed as civilisation advances, its potency should arguably decline, and be replaced by a more co-operative impulse, and this may one day pose an interesting challenge to the market economy.

A centrally-organised command economy, on the other hand, uses a system of centrally fixed prices, production – and demand! But experience has shown the severe structural weaknesses of such a system: it seems to fail the ultimate test, in that it does not work effectively and efficiently to achieve economic activity. Let's look at this carefully.

For a start, there are problems within the system, in that, being production-led, there is either inevitable wastage or else interminable queues, when it is subsequently discovered that demand is different from what was anticipated. Everyone depends excessively upon the motivation, competence and intelligence systems of the central planners. There is an uncomfortable presumption that one person (or group of persons) knows better than everyone else. With central planning, society only has the benefit of the knowledge and intelligence of the governing group, whereas with the self-organisation of the market, it is the knowledge and intelligence of the entire population that is gathered and utilised. The planned economy is the fruit of the labour of the handful of people sitting on the planning committee: it benefits from the power of ten or twenty human brains. A market economy, on the other hand, is driven by individual opportunity, imagination and insight. It benefits from the minds and brains and market intelligence of a million human souls. Not only that, but the market economy is driven by personal, individual motivation rather than by adherence to prescriptive rules and the authority of others. People are doing things for themselves, not just because they have been told to.

Central planners have the immensely difficult task of assessing and forecasting demand, and there is inescapable and wasteful slack in the feedback system for adjustments. By comparison, a demand-led economy is geared to customer need and is therefore more immediately reactive to necessary changes. In such an economy, the mechanisms for price control all work automatically. It is rather like the way experiments have shown that, instead of posting traffic policemen at every junction, it is usually more effective, and cheaper, to leave the vehicles to find their own opportunities to move. No intervention is necessary – the concept follows the 'drive to self-organise' referred to earlier in this chapter. Another problem with a centrally planned economy is that it really needs to be global, or to exclude outsiders from it, so as to prevent damaging interaction with external, incompatible economies. Otherwise, suddenly, home-produced goods have to compete with imports at different prices; exports too then have to compete externally.

It is, therefore, difficult to argue against the market economy as the environment of choice for human society. It is based on the concept of competition, and of course, competition is a universal feature of nature itself. The free-market system does have an excellent theoretical basis: a buyer and a seller will only do business if and when they agree on a price, and, through market pressures, this price mechanism is intended to automatically achieve optimal production levels, optimal variety of goods and services available, and so on. Nobody actually *invented* the idea of the free market – it is simply a formalised observation of natural human behaviour, which is seen to work best in a large diverse market with a diversity of opportunities and free competition with universal knowledge. The theory does get rather distorted in practice, as 'the market' is an imaginary and necessarily global concept, and the critical assumptions of flexibility of individual production and prices – as well as 'market intelligence' itself – are often not a genuine practicality. Moreover, there are some concerns about the inequality that often results from market economics, and arrangements need to be in place to compensate for this: this matter is considered again later in this book. But for the purpose of doing business, we can assume that the free market does deliver results.

What we have now shown is that human beings *need* to do business with each other, and this book assumes that they will do so within the setting of a market economy, for the reasons outlined above. What do we now need to enable business to happen? There needs to be

- an overall economic environment which regulates all business transactions so as to give the participators the confidence to engage in commitments with each other; this is the rule of law and respect for private property;

- a system by means of which exchanges can take place between the different participators; this is the function of 'money' in all its various forms; and

- a means of structuring the co-operative involvement of various different participators into a team or 'enterprise unit', which then co-ordinates their contributions so as to satisfy demand effectively.

The primary requirement is that economic activity cannot take place at all without the existence of *confidence*. We need confidence that rights will be respected and responsibilities honoured. We need confidence not only in the whole of social cohesion but also in the trust necessary for every single transaction we make. Confidence is crucial to business because so much of economic activity involves at least one of the parties to a transaction not getting or doing something on the spot.

You rent a shop or office, and the landlord hopes you will always pay the rent and look after the place; you in turn hope he will always give you quiet possession. You take on staff: you hope that they will work in your interests honestly, diligently and effectively; they hope that you will always pay them regularly, maintain their employment for as long as they are competent, and be a fair and reasonable employer. You sell goods or services to others on credit, and you hope that they will pay you by the promised date. You borrow and hope to be given time to repay; you lend money and hope for a fair return and eventual repayment. You make and promote products, and hope you can get continuing supplies of raw materials.

The overall economic environment needs to be clearly and firmly identified with rights capable of enforcement, so that we all know and respect the rules within which we are going to operate. Yet while all the laws in the land may be there to provide the setting, each individual in the market place must be able to have the confidence that she will receive whatever she has agreed to accept in return for her contribution. For this to happen without swamping the courts with over-regulation, there needs to be a structure to business which fits in with the natural drive to self-organise and which utilises to the full the ordinary nature of human beings, yet which provides some natural balance of power so that automatic market pressures can do the work of regulation as far as possible.

The second requirement for economic activity is that exchanges can take place. For that to happen, we need to have some system of *money*. We then have the means by which different contributions are valued and amounts owing are settled. Cash is the lifeblood of business.

One feature of economic activity that is not always readily noticed by consumers, is that every penny of what they spend goes, ultimately, to other individual human beings. In fact, financial rewards to individuals, whether in the form of wages, dividends, interest or rent, are the *only* cost that business ever has. When a business pays for 'materials', for example, what it is doing is paying some other business, which in turn (ultimately) pays some individual or group of people to physically dig the relevant goods out of the ground (or whatever). And when it pays interest or dividends, the funds ultimately go to the individuals who provide the relevant resources either directly or through their pension fund savings.

What this means is that, while other corporate 'suppliers' are a significant contributor to the economic activity of each specific corporation, nevertheless when the economy is viewed globally, these suppliers disappear altogether as the whole of activity peers right through the various businesses, each of which acts only as a sieve in drawing off the rewards to individuals. It can be seen that, ultimately, individual people receive every penny of sales revenue, and recycle it, subject of course to timing differences due to savings and credit arrangements.

So what do we have? We have a world in which all the necessary energy and natural resources are freely provided. We have the rule of law, and we have a means of exchange. And we have a human population with a whole variety of needs, but also with the propensity to work as a community to satisfy those needs. This self-organisation involves division of labour, and this in turn calls for a structure or framework or mechanism to enable exchanges to take place and to promote the teamwork necessary for larger ventures.

It is this *mechanism* that is the subject of this book.

The business mechanism
So what exactly are we looking for in this mechanism?

We are trying to devise a framework that will not only be the structure within which economic activity may take place, but that will also promote it, motivate it and control it, recognising the personal motivation of each participator. A framework that will give confidence both to those outsiders dealing with it and to those participating within it; a framework that will encourage enterprise within the individual corporation and sustain economic growth collectively; one that will provide an adequate dynamic to create and accumulate economic capital; that will ensure a fair natural balance between the different parties within it; and that will reward each of the parties in a fair and proper way. A framework that will achieve all of this automatically, without too much intervention. This does seem quite a lot to ask, but it is possible!

Before we take the next step forward, we need to return to the question posed earlier in this chapter: *how exactly* do you make business happen?

Empirical observation, i.e., looking at what happens in practice in any market economy, will inevitably conclude that there is at least one person in every single business who motivates the others, as necessary, to engage in doing business. **Business doesn't just happen.** There is always someone, a person or group that is the entrepreneur or motivator, and that person or group of people then brings in others as necessary to build up and operate the business. Even in an established business of some size, the body's organisation and direction is driven and guided by particular contributors who are critical to its success. To be perfectly realistic, the critical contributors initially *are* the venture, and the others are bought in as required from the market.

Whether it's trading, manufacturing, providing services, or even agriculture, the concept of business itself in a market economy comes down to the buying of goods or services from the market, doing something to them, and then returning them back to the market. [By 'market' we mean everyone outside of the business entity that is doing the trading.] Inevitably this involves a surplus or deficit to the business entity, and that surplus or deficit is attributable, and so could be said to 'belong', to those who organised it, those who made it happen. This is a thought that we shall return to, time and again, in this book.

For the present, however, we simply need to accept that a distinctive feature of the market economy is the fact that economic activity results almost invariably in a profit or loss for the enterprise undertaking it. The reason for this is simple: as stated above, each venture involves the buying of goods or services from the market at market price, and then the re-selling of these (with the added value of being suitably transported, re-processed, re-packaged or whatever) back to the market. If you are in business, then both costs and sales revenue (inputs and outputs) are fixed by the external market while the organisation of it all is dealt with internally in your business, with the result that the final sale price of your goods or services bears no *automatic* relationship to the costs you have incurred. If you add up all your costs and compare them to the sale prices you have received, you are bound to have a residual profit or loss on the venture. You buy in something for £5, spend £3 improving or changing it, then manage to resell it for £10, so you make £2 profit. The rights to that residual profit, or the obligation for that loss, are collectively the most valuable aspect of what is known as the 'equity' of the enterprise unit. One reason why it is valuable, is because if you manage to reduce your costs or increase your sale price by £1 (which is just 10% of your sale price in our example), then you increase your profit by 50% (from £2 to £3), and your business is worth half as much again as it was before.

A proper discussion and explanation of *equity* will have to take place in the next chapter, but for our present purposes all we need to accept is that equity (in the sense of the right to the residual profits of a venture and therefore to its ownership and control) is not only an inevitable feature of market economics, it is in fact its driving force. The ability of individuals (whatever the nature of their contribution) to identify with the very business they help to run, and to have personal responsibility for its profits and losses is what makes the market economy work: that is something which we must not lose sight of, as we consider the structure an individual business might best have.

The traditional model of corporate activity in a market economy makes a fundamental assumption that capital is always and exclusively the source of all economic enterprise, and it has to follow from this that economic activity among the general population quite simply does not take place except for the purposes and exclusive benefit of the provider of capital. Now *that* does not ring true.

It is unfortunate that the UK and much of the western world has inherited a form of business organisation (the 'limited company' or corporation), which was devised before anyone thought along the lines set out in this chapter. In the traditional corporation, it was only the provider of capital that really had a worthwhile role. That role was absolutely pivotal – the corporation existed for them – while the role of all the other participators was relegated to that of economic servants, to be paid the lowest possible price, and for whom the potential for self-fulfilment was either purely incidental or else suppressed in favour of the pursuit of the capital provider's own corporate mission. That corporate model has not changed (in its substance) to this day.

It will be clear from this analysis that the form of corporate organisation which we have inherited is not really appropriate at all to present day society. What is needed is a form of corporate organisation, or company, which recognises the reality of human motivation and maximises this for the benefit of all those involved. In so doing, the corporation needs to recognise the economic value of the contributions of the different participators *as participators* in the process rather than as factors to be minimised for the benefit of a single group of participators. This issue is developed in much more detail in the next chapter.

2 The form a business takes: the corporation

Another look at what drives economic activity
We have seen from the last chapter precisely what business is and why we do it. Before we are in a position to decide what form or structure a business itself should have, we need to carefully distinguish exactly what might be the ultimate ambition of economic activity, so that the mechanism of the structure achieves precisely that.

Each of the different participators in business will of course have their own agenda: that is what individual choice is all about in a democracy. One person will want to 'make as much money' as he or she can, so that they can spend it in their own way for the pursuit of their own satisfaction. Another person may simply enjoy the fulfilment of a particular occupation, so long as there is a living wage to keep them going. Some other person will enjoy the satisfaction of organising everyone else, and seeing the venture grow in size and stature. We are all different and accordingly it follows that our individual ambitions are bound to be different. In a modern liberal political environment, business cannot be a matter of simply creating an army of robotic clones of the boss.

Does that mean that business generally cannot have a single identifiable purpose? Not necessarily. To overcome the difficulty of different people having different objectives, we need to ensure that different people can have different types of involvement in their business, and also that they can have some means of expressing and pursuing their views in forming and managing the overall direction of the business. Different people will then be involved differently, and like-minded (or complementary) people will tend to aggregate together to organise their own suitable businesses. This, of course, is what the free market does naturally all the time.

But we have still not identified a single, over-riding primary ambition for business. Those of us familiar with the present corporate model of the UK limited company will be tempted to suggest that the principal purpose of doing business is *to make money* (as was suggested in the simplified proposition in Chapter 1), and they will adduce as evidence the fact that in the present model, the driving force is that the company is owned and controlled by the shareholders who are entitled to all the profits. The only possible motivation one can ascribe to such shareholders is the desire to 'make money' by means of dividends and capital growth in share prices; indeed, every economic or mathematical model of shareholder decision-making assumes precisely that and nothing else.

But how can the ultimate ambition of economic activity (as seen from the perspective of the corporation or of the community) be simply to make money, or to make a profit, for only *one* of the participators in the venture? Unfair inequality must inevitably be the outcome of such a model; and where is the direct link with enterprise? Money and profit are certainly features of trading, they are a means to an end. The problem is that the traditional, and still current, concept that dominates the western world's thinking on doing business, is that it is the provision of capital, and only that, which generates profit. From this fallacy it follows that the resources representing profit always and exclusively accrue to the provider of capital, and are drawn from those without capital. It does not take a great thinker to conclude that the end result of this type of economic activity is bound to be a polarised society divided into *capital providers* and *others*, characterized by ever-increasing inequality, and mollified only by a few exceptionally-talented individuals and by grudging government intervention. The ultimate ambition in doing business – if it is so central to human living – must be more worthwhile than just to add to the stock of capital of those already possessing it.

An alternative view might be that the provision of human labour is all that counts, such as in a workers' co-operative. But this view again is too limited; in concept and in practice it has been effectively discredited politically, and rightly so, as it takes no account of the variety of different contributions which different people provide. Labour itself achieves nothing unless it is organised and inspired and suitably directed; in addition, you cannot do without access to risk capital. The model is as lop-sided as the capital-based model. Business needs *all* types of contribution, the particular assortment varying both from one company to another and from one point in time to another in any one company; the structure of business must be flexible enough to recognise this. In particular, a successful business needs to have directors, or their equivalent, with adequate financial incentives to inspire them.

The pursuit of a policy of low unemployment is certainly a worthy aim, but the problem is that it is so intangible. It is like being determined to be happy, or to fall in love; it just cannot be done to order! Certainly in the market economy you quite simply cannot *make* jobs any more than there being much point in buying in loads of stock in the hope that you may one day sell it. Unless and until you have the customers to buy your goods or services, you just cannot commit yourself to make purchases or engage staff; you can only strive for the conditions under which employers will want to provide more employment. An increase in employment is the *outcome* of successful business enterprise: it follows on from economic success, it does not drive it. It is difficult to see, therefore, how a high level of employment can represent, in itself, the central long-term ambition for economic activity, although clearly it is a welcome by-product.

Let us now look at the primary function of economic activity as we had identified it in Chapter 1: this was 'level one' as described there, namely to obtain, create, process, distribute and service the real resources necessary for human sustenance, comfort and satisfaction generally, i.e., to improve the lot of man by maximising the value to him of the natural resources available. How can we put this more simply? It is to get more goods and more services into more peoples' hands. Surely this has to be the ultimate purpose of doing business, especially if at the same time the rewards of economic activity can be spread as widely and equitably as possible. Now if this is to be the over-riding ambition of doing business, it needs to be framed as a target; it needs to be capable of measurement; success in performance against that measurement needs to be recognised as the foundation of the reward system for all those participating in the venture, all those making it work; and control over it needs to be put in the hands of all those who are most strategic to achieving that target in the success of the overall business.

Economists have of course already recognised the ultimate purpose of doing business, and this is something allegedly achieved by shareholder capitalism. What they tell us is that *economic growth* is what we all need to go for; many in the population would argue that, in addition, this needs to be spread 'fairly'. And what is economic growth? It is getting more products and more services to more consumers – precisely our definition above. Some argue that too much economic growth isn't a good thing. They may be right; but the problem is that it is like saying that too much eating isn't a good thing. The point is, of course, that you need business to produce economic growth – that's its job – just as you need agriculture to produce abundant food. After all, economic growth involves increasing current living standards and satisfying the personal aspirations of individuals. It should also spread the benefits of economic activity as widely as possible, possibly favouring those giving the greatest contribution, and, through tax, contributing to the cost of public services and any support needed for those unable to give any contribution (the poorest and least-advantaged). It is probably creating more jobs, but if not, then it must be evidence of improvements in efficiency, which is also a good thing. At a minimum, it is putting more goods and services into more people's hands, thereby raising their standard of living and, one hopes, redistributing wealth into the hands of those producing it, thereby encouraging them to do even more.

So let's try to get a handle on economic growth. What *exactly* is it? It is normally defined as the year-on-year increase in the gross domestic product, the GDP, of a country or other entity. This in simple terms is the total output of the nation's workforce. For the GDP to rise, this means that there must be more output: this in turn must represent an increase in the labour force and/or an increase in labour productivity. In other words, it is either *more* people working and contributing at the same rate as before, or else the same number doing it, but doing so more efficiently, or a combination of both. How is it measured? In concept, it is a matter of looking at the net outputs of the nation's workforce, or perhaps we should say, the nation's businesses. It is *not* the total sales of all businesses added together, because the purchases of one business are often by definition the sales of another. No, it is the total of what economists would call the *value added*. A business buys goods and services from the market (i.e., from other businesses), does something to them (i.e., adds value), and then returns them to the market (i.e., sells them to other businesses or to the final consumers). The value added is the amount that goes to cover the cost of wages, rents, directors' salaries, other costs, dividends and re-invested profits.

Therefore it would seem to be absolutely ideal for the ultimate ambition of business to be to see a growth each year in the *value added* by each business – automatically giving us economic growth in total – combined with an equitable sharing of the benefits of that value added. At the same time, and this might be quite important, it is ideal for the ownership and control of the value added to be directly in the hands of those most relevant or strategic to the success or failure of the corporation, so that they may decide for themselves the rate of growth they wish to aim for. It is perhaps astonishing that, despite all the talk about economic growth for the nation, and comparisons of the GDP of different nations, until very recently, few companies ever properly measured their *'value added'* and indeed few could do so if required, as there was no recognised or established system for routinely extracting this figure from the accounting records. [National figures for GDP are in fact based on reasoned estimates.] In view of this, we shall need to devise a completely fresh framework or structure for a business to operate within.

The framework for business: the market concept

Devising the framework for corporate activity is not a simple academic issue, not even for lawyers or economists, as it inevitably involves some political effects as well as commercial matters. Why? Because the nature of the framework will not only determine the motivation of the various participants, it will also determine their rewards and it will govern the overall creation and distribution of wealth. In simple language, it decides the way the profits are shared and the power held. But ultimately it will also determine whether or not economic activity will be successful in the medium to long term in achieving its function for society as a whole.

At the end of the previous chapter, we touched on the concept of *equity*. What we saw was that possession of the equity is what provides the possibility for individuals to identify with the very business they run, and to have personal responsibility for its profits and losses. Equity, as it exists as a concept in the present UK corporation, is identified wholly with ownership of the *ordinary shares* of a company. That is why they are sometimes described as the 'equity shares'. These 'ordinary shareholders' own the company, they appoint and dismiss the directors (at least in theory) and they are entitled to all the profits, either by way of dividend or on a winding-up. It can therefore be seen that equity (in a traditional company) has three distinct components:

- the right to the residual profits

- the right to ownership of the net assets, and

- the right to control of the enterprise unit.

It is now clear that, if corporate equity is the driving force of enterprise in the market economy, and if we wish to harness that drive to give us both growth in value added and a fair distribution of its benefits, then we must ensure that this equity is in the hands of those most relevant to the success of the corporation. We must break the existing link between equity and share capital, and create a new type of equity form.

Let us imagine that equity is a commodity available in *equity units*. We must somehow identify the value added by the business with those equity units, and also ensure that they are held by those persons, whatever their contribution, whose motivation is most needed by the business at that point in time. This way the control of the business, its ownership and the financial rewards, will all be in the hands of those people giving the most important contribution to the business.

How might we do this?

Firstly, we have to single out the people most able to promote, organise, manage, inspire and direct the business. In a very small business, it is of course the entrepreneur who conceives the idea, or who sees a need he thinks he can profitably fulfil, and who then either puts in his own funds or provides his own security for the risk capital, on his own if at all possible. He is the 'board of directors'. Only when he has exhausted his own resources, does he then invite the involvement of the other contributories, with all their terms and conditions. He or she is invariably reluctant to 'give away too much of the equity'.

This director (together with the team he may have assembled) can clearly be seen to be at the centre, at the heart, of the corporation from the very beginning, and to want to stay that way: directors constitute the function which is the driving force of the business organisation, which manages, organises, operates, motivates and energises the rest of it. They are responsible for the immediate good or bad day-to-day decisions in a way in which no disinterested employee or government department or central planner could possibly be. We therefore recognise that in those directors (at the start of a small enterprise) is vested the totality of the equity of the enterprise. After all, they started it off in the first place (*not* the shareholders – that was a fiction from before the Victorian era). We then leave it to market economics. The directors recognise that they will need risk capital, they will need critical employees, possibly critical suppliers, and so on. As the need arises, so they bargain with the providers of these other services, and gradually the equity units are parcelled out.

It will be obvious that once the corporation starts to grow, the equity holders may well not all be directors. We then have a position where the directors have the duty to co-ordinate and direct the enterprise – to control it in a day-to-day sense – precisely as they do under the present rules, but there will be a body of persons to whom the *directors* are responsible and accountable for their own performance. Who will this be? This will be the body of equity holders, those who have invested their commitment or pooled their resources at the invitation of the directors, but reserving for themselves the ultimate authority over the enterprise. As under the present rules, the directors take upon themselves the duty of making critical decisions concerning resources which do not necessarily belong to them, as well as the lives and livelihoods (and the social environment and so on) of persons who depend on them: it is therefore necessary that the directors should be accountable to those several persons and – in some way – to be 'controlled' by those affected, acting as a group.

The persons who have the most relevant interest in the conduct of the corporation's affairs must logically be those who stand to gain or lose by its success or failure and whose lives are affected by it. These same persons are likely to be those with the most commitment to the corporation, and it logically follows that the control of a corporation should be in the hands of the same persons who ought to be sharing 'the equity'.

We shall go into much more detail about those who are likely to be equity holders later, but at this stage you may be asking: how do we tie in the equity units to the value added? That again is surprisingly simple, so long as we have the right conceptual idea of what a business or corporation is in a market economy.

To fully understand the idea, we must first ask: what actually is *the market*? It is a large, varied collection of buyers, sellers, consumers, providers, whatever. It is in fact everybody human, plus all the impersonal bodies (or corporations) consisting ultimately of humans – but ***excluding me***. This concept of definition by exclusion is crucial to market economics: **I** (and whoever I am representing, such as my company) am not part of the market, the market is everybody else. **I** am the one who has to somehow deal with the market, with *them*.

But who am *I*? At its narrowest, I am just me, an individual person. At other times, however, *me first* extends to become *my family first*, or my team, my club, or my employer. In wartime, it becomes *my nation*. I identify with what I feel I belong to, and everyone else outside of that circle is the market. We all have an obsession with the concept of personal identity and it is a common observation that it is only when an individual can identify with his own vested interest that he manages others' affairs as if they were his own.

In fairness to mankind, however, there is evidence of awareness of a very extended identity – even, for some, the whole of our planet and the rest of life. Sometimes it becomes a matter of simple contrast: the intensity of the glare of an alien threat reduces the contrast between 'me' and my neighbour, to the extent that we then identify with one another in our common struggle. This would explain man's preparedness to lay down his life for his country. Public spiritedness, charity and a sense of fairness and justice are not odd quirks that are ill at ease with self-interest: they are simply expressions of a wider self-interest, an extended identity. There can be no sense of identity with someone or something you do not understand, but conversely, when you do see and understand the context in which you share existence with others, you can and do identify with them.

Optimism for the future of the market economy rests to some extent upon a greater awareness of the needs and relevance of both the environment and all other forms of life, and the complete acceptance of our mutual interdependence, so that the sense of mutual identity will increase to the level at which logical and practical self-interest replaces any need for altruism. But the fact remains at the present time that market economics depends upon the unbridgeable gulf between the reasoned selfishness of *me* and that of *everybody else*.

What is the relevance of all this lengthy discussion to the corporation? The point is that if the corporation's equity is *me*, then there is a clear distinction between

me: as the equity holders, i.e., the directors, the risk capital providers, the critical employees, all those whose contribution is most important and most valuable (i.e., greater than the price immediately paid), and whose efforts produce the value added; and

the market: as everybody else, whether suppliers, casual weekly staff, temporary capital, and so on – all those who are paid the full market price of what they sell or provide, so that they are in theory relatively replaceable.

In other words, the *equity* of the business must be held by those who are the *critical participators within it*, and who constitute what the business is. The contribution of those participators will be worth more to the corporation than the price they are paid, and the profits resulting are then shared between them (on top of the basic price they were paid for their contribution). It does not matter what was the nature of their contribution: to provide basic risk capital, critical marketing talents, unique inventiveness, quality of human management and motivation, or some other crucial supply or provision. The essence of the matter is that if their contribution was critical to the business, and therefore by definition critical to its generation of economic wealth, then they will have been in a position to bargain with the directors for a portion of the equity – without having to *pretend* that they are capital providers (as present day shareholders do) and artificially dressing up as such in order to justify their share of the action.

It is a fundamental observation of all economic activity that, while some resources may be plentiful, others are in limited supply. The ideal corporate structure should therefore express itself in a way in which the scarcest, and therefore most valuable, contributions to it are likely to be maximised. These scarce contributions might include risk capital, the enterprise of bold, resourceful directors, the drive and organisational talent of senior management, the skills and dedication of the core workforce, strategic suppliers, and willing customers (especially in a monopoly situation). A complication is the fact that the identity, the extent and the relative order of the critical contributions all tend to vary, not only from one corporation to the next, but even from month to month in each corporation. The ideal corporate structure therefore needs to be sufficiently flexible to accommodate this feature automatically. But how?

By at last bringing market economics to the very heart of the corporation.

3 A fresh look at the corporate model

The historical perspective
Let us look first at how we got to where we are today. The existing 'capitalist' model of the corporation is the product of its own historical development. The conceptual framework of capitalism was a natural response to the needs and circumstances of the time, designed to accommodate prevailing social attitudes. The first corporations were formed in the sixteenth century, when our ancestors were just embarking on an age of great discovery and enterprise. We had only just re-discovered the other half of our planet. The supply of desired goods – albeit a long way away – could be said to be overflowing: it was just waiting to be collected; the supply of labour was abundant, servile and of negligible cost; enterprise was everywhere. All that was in short supply was capital; most of this was concentrated in few hands and largely tied up in land and agricultural stock, with little 'liquid' cash around waiting for investment. The greatest demand, by far, was therefore for capital. Little changed in the years that followed. If anything, the position was reinforced, as the projects for which corporations were subsequently required were largely those public utilities that were highly capital intensive, so again the provision of capital was of paramount importance.

This was the world in which the foundation structure for the modern corporation was laid: this, accordingly, was the world that expressed its economic activity in capitalism.

The 'corporation' was therefore a concept designed to manage things like cities (which still use the same title) and foreign colonies: in devising that corporate structure, little heed was paid to any requirements for social accountability, evolving economic relationships, or balanced economic distribution. It was about administration, exploitation, and the supreme power of wealth.

The first 'modern' registered corporations were established in the UK in the middle of the nineteenth century; limited liability was introduced in 1855 and the consolidated Act was passed in 1862. What were the social attitudes at that time, which might have influenced the nature of the corporation as it was being adapted to its current form?

Queen Victoria was newly on the throne, Charles Dickens was writing books, David Livingstone exploring darkest Africa, Charles Darwin publishing his *'Origin of Species'*. The Great Exhibition was at Crystal Palace, Britain the greatest nation on Earth; the underground employment of women, and children under ten, finally prohibited. The news was of the repeal of the Corn Laws, the charge of the Light Brigade, the struggles of cowboys and Indians, the final emancipation of slaves in the southern states of the USA. There were no computers, no telephones, no radio/television, no motor transport. Just the horse and carriage, servants and workers, and the landed gentry. The age of the steam train had barely started.

It could be said that not only economic needs, but social attitudes and circumstances, have changed out of all recognition in the intervening one and a half centuries, and perhaps it is now not before time that we disconnect ourselves from the historical development and freshly consider – objectively and dispassionately – just how the equity ought to be shared and the model structured. Some existing alternative models, such as the John Lewis Partnership, artificially contrive (through a legal trust arrangement) to share the benefit of the equity among the employees, and achieve this very successfully; others, such as the co-operative model, see the equity as being totally due to the workforce or totally due to the consumers, and therefore lack any recognition of the profound importance of the directors and others. Employee representation models give a more significant role to the workforce through various systems of participation, co-determination or simple consultation. This is achieved either through employee councils, worker directors or worker participation models such as the two-tier ('dual') board systems in France, Germany and Holland. But none of these models is suitable for or readily adaptable to all types of small, medium-sized or even large corporations, and none of them have built-in provision for substantial changes, such as in the proportions of the different contributions, or in the marginal sustainability of the enterprise. And none of them provide for *both* a well-motivated and enterprising board of directors *and* an effective and harmonious system of ultimate supervision.

Outline of a new model

Instead of regarding capital providers as the fountain of all enterprise, the proposed corporate model places the directors at the heart of the corporation where they belong. They are its initial promoters, while all the other potential participants, including the capital providers, stand passively in a circle, waiting to be invited in. The directors then act in the best interests of the corporation as a whole (it being at this stage totally in their ownership and under their control) in bargaining as necessary with each new participant so that

1. that particular critical participator is brought securely *within* the corporation

2. their immediate cost is probably reduced as they will share in subsequent profits (this being the purpose of the bargaining) – thus reducing the threshold of economic viability

3. that critical participator has a voice in the ultimate control and direction of the enterprise.

While the directors retain the same role that they have exercised under the traditional model, the shareholders are replaced by a board of 'governors' consisting of the current equity holders or a committee of them. This board will have been actively selected by the directors to create a workable team of those persons most important to the corporation – in dramatic contrast to the haphazard and unwieldy jumble of shareholders to whom directors are technically answerable under the present system.

It follows that, as the equity holders have, by definition, real relevance to the conduct of the corporation's affairs, they will want to be much more actively involved than is generally the case with shareholders. They are not necessarily directors, although it is likely that some of them will have been appointed as such. As equity holders, however, they are likely to welcome the concept of a cohesive and effective working relationship between themselves and the directors in order to maximise overall direction and control. This gives a whole new meaning to active corporate governance, and participation in industry. The 'governors', being either all the active equity holders or a chosen committee of them, would meet regularly, perhaps monthly, with the directors and be involved in all strategic decisions.

Those directors who need, and get, little strategic input from others clearly deserve the lion's share of any profits resulting from their own efforts: as they need to give out little or none of the equity of the enterprise, they therefore keep the equity, the control and the profits for themselves alone.

When a company first starts to trade, the directors are the only equity holders. There is no-one else. It is the equity holders who own and control the business undertaking, and it follows that when the directors need to involve many others as participators, those directors will lose control of 'their' company to the body of equity holders in general, and, as in the present traditional model, will be ultimately responsible and answerable to them. The equity holders or governors therefore not only have a very meaningful role, but have the facility and structure to exercise their powers in a far more relevant and immediately effective way than happens with traditional shareholders.

Equity units

It was suggested in earlier chapters that the equity of a corporation should belong not to the shareholders, but initially to the corporation itself, by being vested in the directors. It has also been indicated that the directors have the duty of co-ordinating the other participators; and finally we have observed that the market mechanism does seem to work in a practical way. It is now suggested that the access to that equity should logically be through the directors themselves, to be available from them for the benefit of the corporation. In their dealings with all the other contributories, the directors will bargain to obtain the best deal for the corporation as a whole – synonymous with the general body of equity-holders. With the directors being initially in possession of the equity, and in a successful company, continuing to do so to a significant extent, there is less conflict of interest such as exists in some of the larger UK companies where the directors may have a different motivation from the corporation as a whole.

Other participators may now bargain with the directors: those providing risk capital will seek a share in the equity, but so will key employees insisting on 'being involved' as a necessary reward for special effort or commitment, and so too may strategic suppliers. If the corporation buys goods off the shelf for cash, then the cash paid is the full price. If the corporation is well established and financially sound, it will probably be able to insist on monthly credit at no extra cost. On the other hand, if there are special circumstances where something extra is needed, for example, extended credit, or the corporation's ability to pay is in doubt, or where the supplier is being asked for special commitment of some sort, such as making a unique item in a special way, then in many of these cases – as in the case of strategic employees, and the provision of risk capital – the contribution by that supplier is one of the many features that help to produce or maintain the special 'equity' of the corporation, and accordingly it follows that a portion of that equity – a slice of the action – might need to be made available to that supplier.

It will now be seen that it is illogical for the equity to be synonymous with the share capital, such that the other relevant participators have to be artificially dressed as shareholders in order to qualify for equity participation. Equity is a separate, valuable commodity to be bargained for among the providers of any of the scarce resources that comprise a modern corporation. This book therefore proposes a new concept: that of *equity units*.

Equity units are a means of notionally apportioning equity control together with current and past profits so as to identify a particular person's portion or 'slice of the action' for a particular period in return for his or her specially valuable contribution. In most such cases, the contributory's contract with the corporation will have been 'executory' (i.e., not completed or executed or paid for, but with *continuing* relevance) in some strategic way, so that the only appropriate way of compensating for this is to give a slice of the action as well as a representative say in the control of the whole business.

It is therefore suggested that a corporation should stand possessed of its equity in the form of equity units. For accounting purposes this will then be apportioned (as a notional record) among the equity unit holders. It has already been shown that it is the promoters/directors who create and co-ordinate the corporation – who drive the vehicle – and therefore they are the logical persons to deal with the issue of these units, to be made available by them to the various other contributories by means of individual or collective bargaining. On this basis, the success or failure of the enterprise, and the fruits of its success, are automatically awarded to all those who have actively contributed to it beyond the mere casual buying and selling of goods and services. The control of the enterprise is in the same relevant hands. By leaving the units to be a matter of bargaining, no complex formula is needed to share the control and the interest in residual profits, or to cope with major changes in the corporation's affairs – it all happens automatically in accordance with the established rules of successful free-market bargaining. And most importantly, those in control identify directly with what value the corporation adds to the market.

One point which will be self-evident is the critical importance of the employees: customer care is something which can only be provided by staff, i.e., it is delegated. In practice it is very rarely the directors and more usually the employees who deal with everyone else engaging with the business.

The equity units are issued for an agreed, limited period of time, appropriate to the contribution to be given by the participator in question. Therefore the participator shares directly in the fruits of his or her contribution. The units would cease to be active some time after the contribution ceased, so that the body of equity holders at any one time represents the current contributors only. A person whose contribution was not likely to yield results for some time, would naturally hold their equity units for an appropriately longer period. This gives expression to the need for a corporation to be flexible – unlike traditional shares, which retain the rights of ownership, control and profit-sharing long after the end of the original contribution which attracted those shares (an artificial permanence exceeding life itself) – and reflects the reality of changing circumstances and trading conditions. It also provides properly and accurately for the distribution of wealth directly to those creating it.

After a person has ceased contributing to the company, his or her equity units will, after a suitable period, cease to be *active*, but they will not be *cancelled* until he or she has received the cash payout representing the share of profits accruing while those units were active. This is easily calculated by the company, which will pay out its dividends when the directors consider that it safely can, systematically reducing the outstanding units earned. Therefore ultimately all equity unit holders will receive precisely their share of profits in cash, the earliest years being paid first. At any one time the company will have a pool of 'equity funding' or retained profits that will be the accumulated profits represented by the most recent equity holders' contributions (plus probably the last few non-active equity holders who have not yet been paid off). As dividends cannot be paid to new equity holders (including the directors themselves) until all the old ones have been paid, the directors and present equity holders have an incentive to pay out the non-active equity holders, this balancing the natural desire to retain as much cash as possible within the company.

Any thoughtful consideration of the nature of present-day share capital will lead to a realisation that its risk profile changes with time and company performance. When first issued, it is likely to be high-risk capital, and therefore deserves a high allocation of equity units, but in a continuing company its vulnerability reduces with time. When this happens in our proposed new form of corporation, it subsequently qualifies for fewer equity units, and this is the source of increasing reward then available to other participators, in particular the management and workforce upon whose efforts the success of the corporation now largely depends. This concept recognises that the corporation is as essentially organic as any other live creation.

Paying wages and salaries in full in cash each week or month may in some circumstances be wasteful and does not involve employees in the vital conceptual feature of participation: if both staff (including directors) and shareholders had smaller payments on account pending the accumulation of adequate cash resources, the corporation would be more powerfully flexible and fit to cope with difficult times. There would be a greater capacity to temporarily reduce total labour costs (in exchange for equity units) without necessarily cutting staff numbers: the marginal labour decision would move from whether marginal revenue exceeded full wage cost (including payroll tax, etc.) to whether it exceeded immediate cash cost. This lower figure obviously means that *more* marginal staff would be employed.

Bonus wages to core employees (i.e., dividends from the equity units) would become an appropriation of profit rather than an expense, so that the provision of productive employment becomes a successful achievement, not a control failure. The employment of a substantial number of core employees can then be seen to be a sign of the success of a corporation; it is involving the community and rewarding it. Under the traditional system, the existence of high wage costs (which are in reality payments to those people adding value to the market) is seen not as something to be celebrated, but as a problem and a burden.

It may be helpful to explain in detail how the proposed new form of corporation may be set up in the first place, and then it should become clearer how the concepts would apply to the subsequent life of a large and complex corporation.

Equity units in practice: setting up a new corporation

A sole trader, of necessity, usually combines most of the 'factors of production' in himself. But he may additionally have to seek loan capital (perhaps from a bank), employ staff and enter into other contractual obligations. The equity, however, remains entirely his, and, with it, the risk of failure. The self-employed businessman (operating under his own name and not within a limited company) is of course personally liable, without limit, to all his creditors, bankers and any other claimants in the event that there are insufficient trading resources to pay them. The fact that there is a limitation to such liability as a feature of the present corporate model is often the negative impetus which encourages small businesses to incorporate (i.e., to trade as a limited company); but this is one aspect of the present rules which can hardly be said to have produced worthy improvements to the general economic situation in relation to such small incorporations.

Once the business enterprise grows, it will develop its own identity. This will be a separate extension from the individual founder, and this identity will reflect in addition the complexity of relationships with employees, customers and suppliers. The business entity (which includes the whole bundle of such relationships) will want to be less dependent on the mortality and active involvement of those who founded it. The enterprise itself, rather than the persons who founded it or who are presently running it, will want to own any freehold or leasehold premises; there will probably be significant suppliers looking for a continuing relationship not wholly dependent upon the existing owner, and perhaps wishing to see publicly-available (and audited) accounts for the venture; there are likely to be key employees anxious for a 'permanent' employer, perhaps keen to have an opportunity to express (in a structured forum) their views regarding the overall development of the business, and to have a 'slice of the action' – and to have sight of the published accounts; and there could be significant capital requirements, for which only an incorporated enterprise (because it does not blur the distinction between business and private assets) can offer the security of a floating charge debenture, and the perceived professionalism of incorporated status with the comfort of an independent annual audit. For all or any one of these reasons, the sole trader/partnership firm (known in the UK as 'self employment') can become unsuitable, although the point must be made that, while the parties mentioned in the previous sentence generally prefer to deal with a corporation, there can be no denying that the limited liability available to the owner/director in the present limited company model is a significant deterrent to these other parties, in many cases leading to a demand for personal guarantees to compensate.

These are some of the reasons which encourage businessmen today to form limited companies. Except for the very smallest of enterprises (perhaps those simply seeking a separate legal entity for a particular aspect of their affairs, something which is probably an abuse of the concept of incorporation) these business people should have reached a decision that, instead of just making some money out of a small business, they want to establish a 'public' entity in their community. Incorporation is then the act of formally recognising that the self-employed wish to enter a completely new relationship with their business contributories. With the existing private limited company concept, the change on incorporation is, for many of the smallest candidates, hardly noticeable and the concept of the company's separate legal identity is either the sole object (to avoid personal liability) or else is little more than an irksome irritation, as is the requirement for auditors and statutory disclosures. In such cases, the small company exists merely as a safer alternative to self-employment: it is a single person's earning source with no regard being paid to social obligations. Incorporation should instead be a fundamental change of attitude by all the business contributories: they are to become involved in the undertaking.

For the smallest enterprises which seek incorporation but do not want all the baggage which that entails, it is suggested that a form similar to the present 'unlimited company' model is probably ideal. They then have a separate legal identity with all its benefits, such as perpetual existence, but need not be burdened by audit costs or the public disclosure of their accounts. If the proposed new form of incorporation is to create an entity which has a worthwhile place in the community, then those seeking to promote it must be prepared to involve more parties more fully in their venture than the 'one man and his dog' concept which has come to typify many of the present smaller private limited companies and given them a bad name as a result.

Let us now look at a typical scenario for the setting up of a new corporation.

Dealing with participators

The proposed system is designed to reflect as far as possible the 'natural' progress of events. One or more persons (the original promoters) have had the idea for a new business, or else they already operate one as a partnership, and they decide that the best structure would be to seek incorporation. At this stage, only the promoters are actually involved. They choose the name and agree among themselves the outline of their plan. They incorporate a suitable 'company'. At this stage the promoters stand possessed of the entire stock of equity units. They have actually *created* the initial equity and embody the totality of it. They then start to add some flesh to the skeleton of their plan and they co-ordinate the selection and collation of the various other participators necessary. They now seek the critical contributions of others to augment the value of their equity, and in return they have to parcel out portions of that now-increased equity to them:

Capital

One of the promoter's family or friends may have some spare capital which he or she is prepared to put at risk, or some personal asset which he is prepared to put up as security for outside borrowing. In return, however, he demands some equity units to represent the genuine risk he is taking. Generally speaking, directors have always been reluctant to have more contributories than necessary, but this is largely because under the present rules the awarding of equity shares at any time for any purpose usually leaves the proportions fixed permanently for evermore, an absurdity that leads to companies having blocks of shares being split up and passed down to children and grandchildren, or else sold to all and sundry. Even so, this reluctance has to be balanced by having adequate capital resources, and in the early stages having adequate capital is crucial. The promoters may therefore also approach an outsider, offering equity units again by way of essential encouragement. They will also discuss their proposition with their bank or another institutional lender at a very early stage, and if borrowings are requested, a financial institution may also request some equity participation in view of the risk inherent in start-ups, although it must be said that clearing banks in the UK are not in the 'risk' business at all, advancing only relatively secure loan capital.

Premises

The business will need premises – either the home of one of the promoters, or a retail or industrial unit, an office, or some other suitable base. It may be that the premises are rented, in which case the landlord will either want personal guarantees from the promoters, or will insist on some equity units, as the new corporate entity has no track record and at present can probably offer little in the way of formal security. The landlord may grant occupation to the company only to find that the rent is not being paid, the premises are not being looked after and there are problems in recovering possession and finding new tenants: equity units would give them some incentive to participate at this stage.

Directors

Normally the original promoters will become the founding directors, but sometimes an additional director with special skills (e.g., a sales or finance director) will be needed, and such a person will join the team and share in the equity units available. The directors are crucial to the success of the corporation at all times, and therefore justify a major stake in the equity, but, being practical, they may have to initially moderate their claims so as to allow sufficient units to be available to those other parties upon whom they depend so heavily at the very start – risk capital in particular.

Employees

Generally speaking, employed staff will want to be paid the full value of their work each week or each month, as there is (initially at any rate) little real security that the employment will continue beyond the contractual period of notice. There may however be key employees whose special commitment is essential and for whom security or involvement is more important as an incentive than simple pay rates. It may not be possible to pay adequate wages at this stage, and equity participation makes up for this. Moreover, once the employees are settled in, it becomes important (economically as much as morally) to avoid capricious and costly staff turnover, and therefore the general body of employees will seek and respond to an element of equity participation. Similar comments apply here as they do for directors: the *initial* allocation of equity units to employees is likely to be a lot less than after the corporation has become established. Experience shows that once a corporation of any material size is properly established, then its continuing success will probably be largely a result of the relationship between its directors and its workforce, and the inspiration, quality and efforts of both. These two parties are of course the principal means of putting proposals into practice, and it is difficult to argue against their justification of a substantial portion of the equity in an established corporation. Employees are obviously paid basic wages for the work they do, as are directors, but the purpose of equity participation is to inspire them to greater effort and commitment. They are all individuals, but they are asked – for the common good – to suppress their individuality and replace it with an institutional identity in the pursuit of a corporate mission: such suppression must be compensated for by an appropriate share of equity participation, so that the individuals are positively motivated to have a sense of *belonging* rather than to feel exploited or sold for a salary or wage.

Suppliers

Most trade suppliers will be content to sell their goods or services for cash or monthly credit, being prepared to accept an element of risk in return for the profit in the sale and the prospect of doing further business in the future. Some critical suppliers, however, may need to be more involved: if the new company's business depends on its suppliers for price, quality or delivery, or if the supplier makes special arrangements (to what would otherwise be his own prejudice) in order to satisfy the particular requirements of the customer company, then some sharing of equity units may be necessary, particularly if an extended period of credit is sought, or if the success of the corporation is likely to be in part due to the special efforts of the supplier. This might even apply in the type of arrangement that exists between a powerful retailer and a relatively small supplier.

Under the traditional model, such a supplier can be in an unequal and unfair relationship with a major 'customer', as a result of which it gets badly squeezed. There are two straight-forward solutions to this under the proposed new model. Either the major customer can have equity units in the supplier (so that there is less incentive to squeeze the margin, as they will both share in the benefits of a larger margin), or the small supplier can have equity units in his major customer (so that he shares some of the benefits that the customer makes out of him).

Customers
Generally speaking, the public will not bargain for any equity participation on the simple grounds that the price paid adequately reflects the value of goods or services supplied. There are exceptions, however, such as when the corporation supplies not the general public but a very small section of the community – such that perhaps just one or two other manufacturers or traders depend on the performance of the subject corporation, and therefore wish to exercise some control in return for the valuable contracts they have given to it. In the case of large corporations, there is also an argument for representation among the equity holders by some relevant consumer group. In fact the technology now exists to achieve this; and it has been put into use in a partial way with the introduction of customer loyalty cards among some large retailers. It is ironic that the principles of the free-market economy should in effect argue that the consumer is 'king', while the existing company law and accounting structure completely ignores the putative king and takes capital instead as their sovereign. The word 'customer' (like 'employee') has been conspicuously absent from every Companies Act. In the case of public utilities, there is a strong argument that consumers should be well represented among the equity holders as it is the consumer public that gives the utility its powerful and valuable monopoly. To be represented on the governing committee would go some way to balancing the otherwise unequal relationship between the two principal parties to the corporation.

Conceptual basis
It will be seen that the use of equity units as the currency in which risk, commitment, and special effort is measured, should enable new enterprises to get off the ground a little more readily by spreading the

benefit of equity participation to all those other contributories who might not otherwise be prepared to help support the new venture. Where the proposed corporation differs again from the present model, however, is that the equity units are made available only while the particular contribution is being made. This concept is crucial, because it means that at the start, units can be given freely to capital providers and others, without the proportions being forever written in tablets of stone; five or ten years later, these units can be redeemed and then re-issued to staff, directors or others as the need arises. This flexibility, which reflects the dynamic nature of a corporation with its ever-changing needs, must be a significant incentive for directors to issue equity units more readily.

Some promoters will perhaps want to keep the entirety of their equity if at all possible, and (subject to any rules of governance which might require mandatory representation among the unit holders of certain classes of contributory such as employees) the proposed corporate model does provide for that. 'All' that the promoters have to do, in addition to being the directors, is to provide all the risk capital and all the commitment, and pay all the other contributories the full value of their contracted contribution: in such circumstances, most of us would consider the promoter to be welcome to virtually all the profits and virtually all the control! Anyone contracting with such a corporation has the opportunity to demand equity units in return for any contribution she makes, and the power lies with the market to ensure that units are made available when they should be. Whatever statutory protection is available, the time-honoured doctrine of *caveat emptor* must remain the primary principle in any free market system.

Essentially, the corporation is designed to work within the market economy; if free market principles are to apply to the trading operations, then they should logically also apply to equity rights as a fundamental part of the bargaining/price mechanism concept. The reward for 'enterprise' and the incentives necessary to promote it, apply in more senses than one: it is not just the directors or the shareholders, but the whole body of participators in a corporation that provides the enterprise and sustained effort necessary. The proposed corporation therefore separates off equity as a valuable commodity in its own right, to be bargained for from the directors by any party with sufficient interest in the corporation, and to be held by them only so long as that relevant interest is strategically important to the corporation. In this way the success of the entity can be seen to be attributable to the corporation as a whole, and this in turn can then be attributed to those participators – whatever the nature of their contribution – whom the directors have had to accept as being critical to the corporation's success: those whose contribution was greater than could be measured by the price immediately paid, simply because the contribution was not available without the attendant equity being offered. This structure also therefore offers the possibility of control to all those seeking confidence in major executory contracts.

Likely outcomes of the proposed new model
If the nation is to achieve economic growth (which is an annual increase in GDP), then what needs to be maximised is the net output of value added by each business entity. In corporate terms, this is the difference between the external turnover (i.e., sales to the market) and the cost of goods and services bought in from the market. It is, quite simply, the work output attributable to the efforts of those participating in the corporation. Those participators generate economic wealth and add value to the totality of the market. ***In the proposed model, it is precisely those persons who will be the equity holders and it will be precisely that value added which they will share between them.*** What could be more ideal? By contrast, with the traditional corporate structure, employment and the paying of wages (even to highly effective employees or directors) is not regarded as a successful achievement but as a negative expense to be minimised. Success is viewed only from the limited perspective of a single participator in the economic process – the original capital investor, who may well have died and passed on his shares to totally disinterested children and grandchildren.

If we re-define 'participator', we can encompass all those whose contribution to the company is strategically important and, generally, greater than the price immediately paid. Thus a participator is a person committed to the corporation, given only a 'payment on account' and therefore one who is an investor for the longer term, and who has therefore been in a position to bargain for a portion of the corporation's equity. Equity is in this case a wider concept than merely the provision of share capital. In terms of practical accounting, we then have a position where the corporation produces a surplus above the cost of bought-in goods and services, and out of this added value makes payments on account to the participators (risk capital, directors, core employees) plus a surplus retained for re-investment pending eventual distribution to the participators. The proportion of units each participator has in the total equity would be a matter of individual free bargaining between that participator (or group of participators) and those at the heart of the corporation – the directors – whose job it is to promote, co-ordinate, direct and manage the entire corporation. Those equity participators would be the body of persons most concerned in the corporation's affairs and therefore most relevant to exercising the notional 'control' function currently assigned to equity shareholders. Once their contribution ceased, however, they would cease to hold 'active' equity units.

What would be the specific outcome of these proposals?

1. The measure of success becomes the growth in total value added, i.e., net output of economic wealth. This should lead to real economic growth rather than a mere improvement in share price resulting from a higher rate of return on share capital.

2. Additional wages to core employees become an appropriation of profit rather than an expense, so that the provision of productive employment is a successful achievement, not a control failure.

3. Core employees are involved in the vital conceptual feature of participation: if employees (including directors) and shareholders have smaller payments on account pending the accumulation of adequate cash resources, the corporation becomes more powerfully flexible and viable in difficult times.

4. There is greater capacity to temporarily reduce total labour costs without necessarily cutting staff numbers: the marginal labour decision would move from whether marginal revenue exceeded full wage cost (including payroll taxes, pension contributions, etc.) to whether it exceeded immediate cash cost. This lower figure suggests that *more* marginal staff would be employed.

5. A move away from the feudal master/servant relationship for permanent employees, towards the concept of true participation, with a handful of non-core employees having the benefit of

genuine free-market exposure. The non-core workers would have individual work contracts providing for specific employment for a specific period, freely bargained for with union support. As these are the marginal employees (by definition), the benefit of a legally-binding six-month contract might well be more attractive than the alternative of unemployment. Each party would at least know exactly where they stood.

6. The directors would be acknowledged to be at the heart of corporate activity, where they belong, bargaining with all the strategic contributories to obtain the best for their corporation, and openly receiving the equity rewards themselves. Their reward and their incentive would be precisely the same as that for capital providers and for the core workforce: all parties would be on the same side.

7. The economic structure of corporations would be revised to remove the artificial permanence of ownership by capital providers, replacing it by more relevant ownership by those strategic contributors able to bargain for a share in the equity of value added while they give that contribution. By identifying equity as a broader contribution than just risk capital, encompassing instead all the strategic providers of 'value added', motivation and reward become based upon adding value to total market outputs, i.e., generating economic growth and rewarding all forms of enterprise and effort, rather than simply redistributing profit to historic possessors of capital.

8. Instead of being vilified, the business community would be appreciated for its efforts to promote economic growth. A key outcome of the new model is that the more successful a company becomes, the cheaper would be its cost of capital (i.e., the servicing cost of its risk capital). This then enables a greater surplus to be shared among those producing it. By contrast, under the existing model, the very opposite happens: the cost of capital rises as the company gets more successful. The share price goes up and so dividends have to rise – and to make that happen, all the other participators in economic activity (those

actually producing the surplus) have to be squeezed more and more, creating grossly unfair inequalities.

9. There would be an automatic redistribution of wealth, but only to those actually generating further wealth and away from those simply leaving it idle.

4 Capital

The participators in the enterprise unit
We have referred to the 'participators in economic activity' and to the 'contributors' to corporate business. Who exactly are they? Classical economics has a concept to which it gives the title 'factors of production'. The fullest list of such factors or participators, or contributors to economic activity, may be identified as follows, using the various names under which each may be known for different purposes:

- Promoters/directors/entrepreneurs/management/businessmen

- Risk capital/shareholders/venture capital/investors

- Loan capital/bankers/investors

- Employees/staff/workforce/labour/junior, middle and senior management

- Trading suppliers/creditors/wholesalers

- Customers/consumers/general public

- Economic environment/national infrastructure/general business confidence/taxation

These are the parties, the collection of whose differences is needed to achieve economic activity. Any one person may of course represent more than one category at the same time – we can all be consumers at the same time as being employees or trading creditors as well.

That is the conventional view. If we think about the basics for a moment, and look at it in a different way, it will become obvious that the only *real* factors of production are the world's natural resources and mankind. If we ignore Nature for a moment – as that is available to us free – that leaves just mankind. In this sense, therefore, the list of factors of production simply comprises individual people performing their appropriate roles in what might be called the 'multiplication' of labour into an integrated economic unit. The creation and organisation of economic activity becomes a matter of selecting and collating the individual participators and bargaining out the rewards necessary for each. Pretty obvious, really.

We saw earlier, in Chapter 1, that economic activity is ultimately all about the interactions of individual people. It is individual human beings that extract minerals from the ground, or that design and build the machines that do it for them; it is, ultimately, individual human beings that build every machine and every structure, and every little part that goes into every next process. Some people provide their labour in the form of enterprise, ideas, connections, motivation and organisation; others provide knowledge, talents or skills; and others provide just themselves. Technology, communications, infrastructure – all these have ultimately been produced by simple human labour. Originally capital itself was created by accumulated labour (although this is discussed further below). It can therefore be seen that, if we set to one side the matter of the overall environment, then all the factors are simply people acting their different roles and providing their different personal natures and abilities and resources in accordance with the principle of division of labour.

How do we now reconcile this with the classical list of factors of production as set out above? Easily – except for one item: capital. So what exactly do we mean by capital? Capital is a somewhat confusing word that seems to have different meanings in different contexts. It is explored in more detail later in this chapter, but for our present purposes, we have to say that, whatever the nature or quality of its source (which could be inheritance, discovery, gambling, gift, theft, or even pure savings!), it is of course the nature of its application that is relevant to us in economic activity, as it is only this latter nature which permits it to qualify as a factor of production. It is difficult to see how its application can be anything other than either one or both of the following:

1. As a stock of cash or working capital, it is the means of paying an exchange value for goods and services produced by others, and of holding necessarily different levels of these while integrating the overall process (i.e., the economic arrangements necessary to cope with division of labour).

2. As real capital resources, it is the 'capitalised' value of past human input (labour, enterprise, organisation, etc.). We have already seen that human labour applied to the products of Nature produces absolutely everything in the economic world, but the problem we have is that modern industry requires a very long chain of processes. We cannot sell motor cars, for example, until we have produced metal from minerals in the ground, produced machine tools and other technology to then make the machines that make the cars, built factories to house them, roads to drive them on and fuel to power them. From start to finish, however, the total cost is only for human effort.

There is, perhaps, a more subtle aspect to this distinction: capital of type (1) is simply the system by which a group of people work productively within one 'layer', i.e., achieve the provision of current sustenance for themselves, whereas real economic capital of type (2) is a system of adding many *more layers* so that production and distribution can become more efficient and productive with each successive layer.

Economic capital cannot be created without the concept of saving. There *has* to be an excess of production over consumption – an investing of input, or an abstinence from consumption – so that the output products of one industry can then be applied as inputs to the next, and so on.

Economic capital is to business what a library of past knowledge is to education and research. At a low level, you may be able to do without it, but you cannot get very far in education without the benefit of the work done by those who went before you. Like a student's access to a good library resource, economic capital dramatically speeds up the process of industry and commerce. Layer upon layer of business can be set down so as to eventually build up a sophisticated and highly productive economy, ultimately utilising a high level of capital investment: a feature of which developing countries are chronically aware.

A library is a bank of capitalised knowledge. The library does not create knowledge itself, nor does it own the fruits of labour of the person using it; it is not consumed by its use – it is only *borrowed* and then returned for recycling again and again. In the same way, real economic capital is the accumulated product (or 'capitalisation') of earlier labour and enterprise; and it needs to be made available for use for (generally) limited periods. We can now see that the factors of production stripped to their barest essentials are simply human beings in both 'present production' and 'past production'.

What we now draw from this is that individual factors of production do not *create* any wealth by themselves, it is the overall corporate economic activity (i.e., their engagement with others in an organised team) that generates wealth, and that to increase this wealth it is necessary for the 'capital' that results to be constantly reinvested within corporate activity. The more intensive use that is made of a library (particularly the adding to it of further titles), the better; similarly, the repeated repayment and recycling of risk capital, while at the same time trying to add fresh knowledge to the library (i.e., to retain economic wealth within corporations) would seem to be the ideal. It is precisely these dynamics which the proposed model must create if it is to be successful.

How does capital produce income?

We have already seen that capital is not quite as simple a concept as might appear to the layman. It could be defined as a stock of wealth, but that is a somewhat circular definition – for, what is wealth? A practical concept of *real* economic capital might be based on a Robinson Crusoe-style view that the saving of income, less consumption, results in an accumulation of goods which can then be applied productively as capital either to bridge periods of low income (e.g., keeping a stock of fish) or to generate greater income (e.g., taking time off to build bigger nets for more successful fishing). Not all wealth, however, is the product of careful husbandry. Much of the world's capital, or should we say, the ownership of it, derives not from earnings but from what might seem to be little more than arbitrary or capricious allocations of entitlement resulting in turn from fortuitous possession of natural resources, from rights allocated within human society, by inheritance, by gift, or by forceful possession. Ownership and inheritance are of course entirely human constructs – a convenient device agreed by most societies for the benefit of some or all of the people within them. It is, however, not the source or ownership of capital that matters to business, so much as its availability and the use to which it is put.

Capital is, to put it mildly, rather useful in business, and can be extremely productive. It does not, however, normally have any subjective or intrinsic *income* potential of its own. To a lone man on a desert island, a saw, a knife and a fishing net are worth everything; yet a bar of gold, a bank passbook and a share certificate are entirely worthless. To a person in the city, the reverse is the case. In terms of natural or real capital assets, these have practical *utility* value, subject to individual circumstances. In terms of *economic* capital, the value of this depends entirely on social rules and market demand – its value lies in the power of exchange. The market, as we all know, always seems to have a scarcity of capital, and accordingly, capital is always in demand and therefore attracts a price – the rate of return for borrowing it or renting it.

These are all basic economic facts which have been well established for centuries, yet they clearly illustrate that, in economic terms, capital itself has no intrinsic income potential unless it is specifically put to use, or the market (i.e., somebody else) wants the use of it to enable them to apply it productively. It is therefore, strictly speaking, a misconception to suggest that, in a corporate sense, "capital produces income": capital made available to a corporation (or to any other business entity) may well enable that entity to produce more income, and if it does, then that capital may be serviced or paid for by passing income back to the person lending it. No bank would pay interest on deposits unless other persons or enterprises were in turn prepared to pay the bank for borrowing those funds in order to use them productively. Indeed in recent times there have been suggestions of *negative* rates of interest applying in circumstances of deflationary prices: you would have to pay the bank to look after your money, because it is better spent now than in the future.

Profit or income does not therefore automatically derive from capital: profit is something earned from *outside* the enterprise unit by means of employing capital and other contributories *within* it. As a further example, it is well accepted that a 'capital injection' into a business is likely to lead to an increase in profits and the generation of wealth. But just for a moment imagine the outcome of a 'labour injection': a proposal that everybody in England should decide not to take off *every* Sunday, but instead to work, for nothing, one Sunday a month. Because labour is ultimately the sole cost of everything, there would be a sudden, tangible increase in wealth generation – even theoretically an annual growth in GDP of almost 5 per cent – without a single penny of capital being involved. There would be 12 more working days at the same labour cost as 250. This does, of course, depend on all businesses being able to make use of (i.e., apply productively) the extra labour time, having no other additional costs, and finding customers prepared to buy the increased production or other output.

It is the whole of corporate activity, the entirety of all that a business does, that generates profit, not the simple provision or application of a single contributory.

This conclusion is important, as it helps to explain why the simple provision of capital should not of itself give rise to the ownership of subsequent business profits. This misconception is entirely attributable to the distortion created by the existing corporate model. It leads to a great deal of woolly thinking in the realm of investment analysis: even such common expressions as 'the return on capital' can now be seen to be no more valid an overall economic assessment of corporate performance than the return expressed in terms of any other scarce resource such as sales area, retail unit, customer or employee.

Risk capital

This chapter is attempting to explore the nature of capital as employed in a business enterprise. The word capital in this context is intended to refer to risk capital or venture capital, as opposed to secured or long-term loan capital or bank facilities. It could be referred to as 'ordinary share capital' because that is the name by which this particular type of capital is currently known in the context of the present UK limited company.

Share capital is the capital attributable to the shareholders of a limited company. It may consist of cash subscribed by them (or by their predecessors), or it may be consideration (i.e., payment) for the value of other goods or services they or their predecessors have provided, or part of it may be a 'capitalisation' of earlier profits made by and accumulated within the company. Share capital is sometimes divided between ordinary (or equity) shares – which are regarded as the real risk capital – and other shares such as preference shares, which are somewhat less at risk.

The classical theory of the incorporation of a new limited company suggests that the shareholders group together with their venture capital and invest it in a new company, subsequently selecting and appointing the directors to make whatever money they can out of it. The capital is generally assumed to be permanently sunk into the company, with the anticipated return being by way of cash dividend out of future profits. The amount of the share capital is intended to be the full amount of the real risk capital, so that any other cash funding requirements may be more easily and readily provided by temporary borrowing from banks and other lenders, arranged by the directors. While the company is in operation, the shareholders (with some exceptions) do not generally expect to get their capital back – although they can, and frequently do, sell their rights to the share capital to others – but instead hope to receive the residual profits by way of dividend once or twice a year.

The availability of risk or venture capital is critical to business enterprise. Virtually all new business ventures need capital of some amount to enable them to start off – some need huge sums – and there can be little doubt that capital invested in a new venture is very much at risk. The availability of private venture capital (as opposed to public or state funding), and the readiness of its providers to put it at risk in business ventures, has been a key contributor to the success of the free market economy in the developed world. It is, of course, not just the very wealthy who invest in venture capital, but a great many ordinary people who put their savings, their life assurances and their pension contributions into institutions which in turn are the greatest investors in the country's industry and commerce.

At the commencement of an enterprise, there can hardly be any doubt as to the speculative nature of ordinary share capital. The cash put in as share capital at the start of a new venture is in the first line of attack if the venture, so far untried, falters. The moment that the cash is subscribed, it is irretrievably sunk in the sense that you cannot ask for it back, and the only return is if either (a) the venture is a commercial success and produces some dividends, or (b) someone else is prepared to buy the shares, or indeed the whole company, from you. [You may also just possibly get some of it back on a winding up of the venture, but only if it was a success.] That is what traditional share capital is all about: failure is, after all, normally understood in terms of *economic* loss – and this means cash loss for the shareholders. So, shareholders obviously deserve a massive allocation of equity in order to have adequate control over their investment and to reap the rewards of their gamble....

But is the argument really as simple as that?

The risk profile changes

It is a proper conclusion, from an examination of what happens to new ventures, that risk capital at the start of an untried enterprise certainly does demand and deserve a lot of equity participation. But that, however, is not a full examination of the complete story: what remains to be questioned far more closely is the nature of risk capital once an enterprise becomes established.

As soon as a new company has completed its first few years of trading, the fearful uncertainty that grips all the contributories at the start begins to disappear. Initially the venture is untried and untested and relies solely on projections, personalities and consultants' reports; as every professional banker and investor will acknowledge, hopes and prospects at this stage need to be heavily discounted. But once the corporation has survived the first few years, there is a track record, an objective historical account, both of the corporation itself and of the inter-related workings of all its participators, as well as direct practical experience of the targeted market place. Upon this foundation, future projections can be based far more reliably. If the entity has come successfully through this initial period, then its ultimate survival is much more assured and the share capital begins to be at far less risk than it was at the very start.

The second feature of a company which has completed its first few years of trading is that – assuming, as we need to, that it has been successful so far – it will quite possibly have accumulated a little bit of fat in the form of reserves, so that there is something for potential losses to eat into first before the initial (subscribed) share capital itself is at risk. Clearly, if the company has not been profitable in these early years, then its future is still very much in doubt: for the purpose of this chapter, therefore, we need to consider only the successful companies as it is the position in *continuing* companies which is being considered.

To pursue this analysis further, an examination of the balance sheets of well-established companies will, in general, show that the actual amount of monetary liability represented by the share capital, i.e., the actual cash received by the company for its own productive use from its share issues, is often dwarfed by accumulated reserves, quite apart from working capital facilities and loan capital. In fact, in terms of fresh funds required for expansion in existing companies in the UK, on average, something like 50 per cent comes from retained profits and 30 to 40 per cent from working capital, leaving just 10 to 20 per cent being provided by fresh issues of share capital. [The position is even more dramatic in other leading industrialised countries, particularly Germany, Japan and the USA, in which corporations have on average retained a far greater proportion of their earnings than in the UK, and therefore depend even less on either original or fresh share capital for funding.] What this means is that in many cases it may actually be a practical proposition for the risk capital (i.e., the amount of share capital originally paid into the company by the shareholders) to be repaid to them, perhaps in instalments, out of accumulated reserves or secured borrowing. You could then say that, in such cases, share capital is no longer absolutely needed. Where does this leave the proposition that the shareholders are always entitled to all the residual profits? This is obviously a sweeping generalisation, but it is clearly reasonable to suggest that, for a successful company, share capital is not really risk capital for much longer than the early stages of its life.

The classical model of the corporation can now be seen to have features in common with the classical Newtonian paradigm in theoretical physics – in that the share capital is regarded as the mechanistic force required to establish the corporation, which is then kept in permanent sustenance by inertia, owing its everlasting debt to that initial force, and providing it with income and capital growth for evermore. In reality, however, the corporation (being a framework for *living* contributories in a *living* world) has as much of an organic, evolutionary and dynamic nature as other living beings, and the permanence of this static debt to initial capital is unreal. In the family unit, the parent has to initially nurture her totally dependent child, but when that child matures, the relationship gradually changes completely until it actually reverses – and, in a similar way, the 'equity' nature of share capital changes upon the maturity of the corporation and (usually) eventually becomes repayable.

It is for this reason that, in our proposed new model, while a very large portion of equity will often and inevitably be bargained for by the share capital providers at the start of the venture, so that they may exercise a major part of the control and accrue for themselves much of the fruits of risk in the first few years, nevertheless after five or ten years or possibly longer, the position will almost certainly be different. At this stage, if the corporation is successful, then quite probably a new contract will be offered by the directors to the capital providers, offering them a lower rate of return and/or a reduced proportion of the equity (in line with the reduced risks they now take, and possibly coupled with proposals to start to repay some of the capital), so that more equity units are available for those other contributors upon whose efforts the continuing success of the corporation now depends.

As the corporation begins to settle down, and the initial atmosphere of inspiration and sheer risk is converted into sustained organisational discipline, drive, commitment and sheer hard work, the emphasis for equity participation and reward is likely to move from the capital providers, who have now done their principal job, to those human beings who are now charged with the duty of putting the corporate plans into practice and making them a sustained reality: the directors and the workforce. It would seem logical that a structural reward system, quite separate from the blunt and unwieldy mechanism of wages (with its unsatisfactory requirement for immediate cash payment), be in place for the strategic contributories as the corporation grows. In addition, some of the suppliers may insist on equity units in those cases where their particular sustained contribution is material to the corporation's success; and so on. A high level of equity being held by capital investors might become symbolic of the immaturity of a corporation, unless it is a highly capital-intensive and rather risky one. It can therefore be seen that the proposed model accommodates the changing nature of the corporation: the theory being that control at any one time will be in the hands of those most relevant to the corporation's present and future, rather than its past.

The rate of return
It can be seen from the amount of capital invested through the Stock Exchange that there is no shortage of capital for investment, and with the increasing recognition of the need to provide adequately, through

private schemes, for retirement and later life generally – and the resulting growth in institutional funding, with their massive inflow of premiums for investment – this is likely to continue indefinitely.

It will also be readily observed that for most of the established public companies, the quoted share price is greater than its original issue price, even after taking account of inflation and any share premium on issue. There is an oft-quoted maxim that says precisely the same thing: that over the medium to long term, the growth in share price should outstrip inflation. There are, of course, many component parts to the increase in share price, but generally speaking, while the share price is a reflection of market perceptions and the laws of supply and demand in shares, nevertheless, underneath it all, there is supposed to be an underlying foundation that a share represents a proportionate 'share' in the company's net assets, including goodwill. In other words, a *share* is both the original investment plus the retained profits attributable to it (i.e., a share in the company's net worth), *plus* the market's perception of the future prospects of the company.

As a successful company will usually retain some of its profits each year, this means that the subsequent value of a quoted share is, in general, significantly greater than the current real value of the funds originally invested for the company's use, while in the meantime, dividends are paid (as a yield *on that higher value*) in order to continue to service the original capital. It must be said, of course, that a portion of those retained profits, certainly in the early years, does represent the balance of a fair reward for risk capital and inflation, after the payment on account which the dividends represent: but another portion represents something else.

Let us look for a moment at one feature of the stock market which appears to be accepted without challenge: the presumption that, *as the share price rises, the required rate of return paid on the original investment also needs to be increased.* This presumption, which is critical to stock market pricing and yet is probably the single most damaging feature of capitalism in its distributive effect, does actually run counter to logical argument. If you consider the directors to be at the heart of the company, organising its affairs in the best interests of the company as a whole, then once the company is seen to be well-established, so that the share capital is no longer at such risk, the cost to the company of servicing its risk capital funding should reduce, not increase. The error lies in the presumption that both the heart of the company and its best interests lie not within the company itself, but with its external shareholders.

One effect that is the result of this damaging perspective is the necessary implication that a large proportion of the cash freshly invested in the stock market does not actually go into industrial and commercial concerns at all but back to the capital providers – and their intermediaries – as extra profit in the form of growth. Just think about that for a moment: when the stock market boasts a 'market capitalisation' for its hundred largest companies of £1,750 billion, around 90% of that never actually got invested in industry at all. When you get your broker to invest £1,000 'on the stock market' (i.e., in existing shares), you are not directly adding anything whatever to the funds available to industry, you are paying a series of past anonymous 'investors' a total of £900 profit to transfer to you the right to the £100 that the first one of them originally invested in industry some years ago. Commerce and industry got 10%; those with existing wealth to invest (and of course, pension funds and other institutions) get the other 90%: that is the contribution of capitalism to economic inequality.

An examination was made of the balance sheets of the top hundred UK companies constituting the FTSE 100 index in October 2014, with comparative figures for a similar exercise in October 1992 [source: *London Stock Exchange*]. The total market capitalisation was taken as being the sum of the market values (broadly the number of shares issued, multiplied by quoted share price) of each of those one hundred companies as at that date, and the cash originally invested in the companies was taken as being the sum of all their issued share capital, plus any share premium account, as at the most recent balance sheet date. The intention is to give a broad indication only, as these figures are necessarily very approximate. They have not been adjusted to exclude the effects of inflation, which would of course be substantial; but neither do they include the cash dividends paid, which would go some way to cover that inflation. The figures also do not exclude the effect of capitalisation (bonus) issues, nor the costs of share issues – both of which would marginally reduce the cash actually reaching the companies.

What this analysis does show, however, is that, on average and ignoring inflation, out of every £1,000 in value of current investment in the biggest companies of British industry and commerce, just £100 (or *barely one-tenth*) was the sum of money actually placed at risk for productive use within industry and commerce, and £900 (or *nine-tenths*) is the profit so far receivable on it *in addition* to the dividends paid. [The equivalent figures for 1992 suggested a current value then of £1,000 represented an original investment of £140 (or *one-seventh*). This would suggest that, on this very rough and ready basis, the situation has not improved.]

A similar analysis of those top one hundred companies, carried out at the same time, showed that the average annual rate of dividend shown in the latest accounts as payable to ordinary shareholders was 48.7%, net of basic rate tax (and therefore equivalent to 54.1% per annum gross under the tax regime then current), when expressed as a percentage of the average share capital (in historic prices) *actually employed* in each case. This suggests that the average gross rate of return actually paid at present as dividends on the funding originally received (in historical cost values unadjusted for inflation) by UK companies is something of the order of 54% per annum, quite apart from the amount of capital growth of 900% (i.e., £900 on top of £100) referred to in the previous paragraph.

This really is difficult to justify. Expressed in less academic language, traditional shareholders as a group invested £100 in a portfolio of shares in the largest UK companies, and now their capital is worth £1,000; in addition, they have been receiving dividend income on their investment throughout, currently expecting and getting a return of over 50% a year on their original investment. What matters of course is where all this generosity comes from. It only arises because the corporate framework squeezes everything it can out of the efforts of all the other participators in the corporation – the workforce, the large and small suppliers, the consumer – for the sole advantage of one participator, the shareholder. This is polarisation masquerading as economic growth.

Seen from this perspective, the problem would seem to be that the cost of capital is based on the wrong figure: the company is having to pay a fair return on the current share price (something quite external to the business) rather than on the actual venture capital funding (within the business) of which it has had the benefit, so that as companies succeed, their cost of capital rises instead of falling.

What happens in practice, however, is that an increasing amount of reward accrues to the capital providers, both in terms of capital appreciation and an inequitably increasing rate of dividend.

One advantage to a company in having a strong share price is of course that the higher the share price, the more the company can then raise, more easily, from a fresh issue of shares. In this situation, however, a company with similar success but structured on our new model would gain precisely the same advantages by simply publishing the facts about its performance and prospects: it does not need an externally set share price to establish this.

The analyses referred to above all relate to the largest UK companies that dominate our economy; but the principles can be seen to be just as true for the smallest private companies and all those in between. Many of the smaller private limited companies have balance sheets showing issued share capital of £100, or even just £2, yet gross assets and liabilities in terms of many thousands of pounds. It becomes an absurd distortion of reality and rationality to suggest that the provider of £2 share capital – often in practice written off to a director's loan account and so never even actually physically *paid* into the company – should thereby own and control all the worth of the company. In such companies it is probable that the same individual *should* own and control the company, because he or she probably does all the work for it, but if that is the case, then the right to ownership and control derives from the individual's contribution as director and as employee, but not as capital provider. The model really must be flawed for such an absurdity to have to exist.

Corporations *do need* risk capital investment funds, and all sorts of institutions and insurance companies and other equity investors have such funds looking for investment. That won't change. What would change under our proposals is that the rate of return on those investments will vary more directly with the risk profile of the actual investment made, rather than with public perceptions of the state of the overall *investor's* market, i.e., it will depend on the investors putting in rather more effort to see their investments managed and constantly recycled. Leaving investments idle for year after year won't any longer be the way to accumulate more wealth.

The enterprise economy
Many of those who deal with the affairs of smaller businesses will acknowledge – if you ask the businessmen directly, they will routinely tell you – that among their greatest difficulties, especially in starting up, will always feature (a) access to capital without

security (i.e., risk capital), and (b) getting paid by customers (debtors). The second problem is made infinitely worse when customers go bust, when the debt is not just paid late, but never paid at all. This issue is related to the whole question of limited liability, which is addressed later in this book. With regard to the first problem, that of raising capital for smaller businesses, it must be said that in many cases there will be weaknesses in their proposals, in their planning or in their personality: but, apart from those with very small capital requirements, or where the promoter already has adequate resources of his own, the availability of venture capital will often be insurmountable and condemn the project before it is born.

Over the last few decades, much political energy, and not inconsiderable public money, has been added to the proposals of some economists that encouragement should be given to the establishment of new small businesses – what has been called the enterprise economy. Yet few practitioners in this field will be able to report that capital-raising for new private companies has become any easier.

It is suggested that where the present system fails is that too much of the venture capital available has been left in established companies where, as indicated above, it is not always absolutely needed, and yet is lavishly serviced – leaving little incentive to invest in new and therefore riskier companies. [Stock Exchange investment may be routinely described as slightly risky, but that is because the resale market for the share is volatile, rather than because the company invested in is likely to fail. The underlying capacity of the company to repay its share capital at the price originally subscribed is rarely at issue, especially if it is well established: in that much more realistic sense, Stock Exchange investment is barely risky at all.] If, on the other hand, the *temporary* nature of venture capital were recognised, then more of it might be available because it could be recycled after five or ten years. The capacity of existing industry and commerce to begin to repay its original risk capital can be seen more clearly if the dividend yield (the rate of return actually paid for capital) is expressed as a percentage of the cash actually invested in the subject company rather than on the basis of the distended current share price. Moreover, in established companies, it should be possible to gradually replace valuable and expensive risk capital by less expensive, secure, long-term investment funding, thus releasing true venture capital for recycling elsewhere.

There is a pressing need for the structured availability of equity funding for new and small businesses: not to throw money at them, nor to make them the subject of complex tax avoidance schemes, but to have some form of professional but market-driven 'equity bank' or venture capital source to rigorously assess the practical commercial potential of new, or young, or needy businesses, and then introduce potential risk capital providers – linked, perhaps most importantly, to suitable equity governors to attend monthly meetings and guide the business to independence.

In the proposed model, if the Government were keen to be seen actively intervening in the promotion of enterprise (although many practitioners and economists gravely doubt whether such intervention in the free market ever achieves the real worth of the money involved), then there is at least a structure which it might find suitable for targeted fiscal incentives: some tax concession, or financial grant, linked to the possession of equity units, such that those making a particular contribution to the promotion or successful continuance of corporate activity could accept a smaller *contractual* payment – thus increasing the corporation's chances of surviving – in return for other benefits in holding equity units.

Financial independence

If we return to the basic purpose of the establishment of an enterprise unit as set out in Chapter 1, it is to enable economic activity to take place for the benefit of all the parties to it. Those who are contributories to it are anxious to see it succeed, because in that economic entity or corporation they can see their present and future employment, or the sustained provision of their economic needs, or the sustained demand for their products or services. For them, the 'success' of the enterprise is in its simple continuance.

Once we abandon the tyranny of the call for an ever-increasing share price, we can see that the success of a company is not interminable growth, or the constant pressure to remove wealth from some participators to hand over to the shareholders, nor the complete domination by one company of the entire market. No: it is simple survival or sustainability, together with adaptability to change – adapting, that is, to the ever-changing trading environment. Success for the participators in a corporation is not necessarily dramatic and relentless growth, nor the bearing of enormous fruits by way of cash surpluses, but simply sustained existence together with sensitivity and flexibility to external pressures, adapting to change as needed; and one of the fundamental elements needed to achieve this, is the possession by the corporation of adequate financial resources.

It is only natural that people are impatient to see their share of profits, but it is equally instinctive for directors to try to resist this. The importance, in the long term, of saving and re-investing can never be over-estimated. Among the internationally-recognised features that are thought to give corporations real competitiveness and economic strength, and the solid ability to withstand temporary depressions and set-backs, are both sound management (in pursuing research and development, in education and training, awareness of customer needs and market trends, etc.) and heavy re-investment in a secure capital base (lack of debt, the use of modern technology, and fully maintaining and upgrading all capital assets). It is clear from this that re-investment is critical to the achievement of the principal objectives of the corporation, and therefore the desire to pay out profits early must be resisted.

It must therefore be welcome and proper to see that, in the proposed model, there will be a powerful impetus for the directors of a corporation, not only in its early years, but at all times, to achieve financial independence – and then to preserve it – by keeping the tightest possible control on unnecessary expenditure, and by keeping any dividend payments to the equity unit holders to such an amount as is clearly surplus to present and projected cash requirements. This impetus derives from the natural desire of the directors to claim back for themselves as soon as possible any equity units unnecessarily held by outside capital providers. It also derives from the fact that equity units are quite different from shares: shareholders constantly want to see their share values rise, and part of what causes this is a high rate of dividend payment. So companies are *urged* to pay out dividends. Equity unit holders, on the other hand, care more about the future of their company than about the potential to sell their interest in it.

Where does that leave us in relation to the capital providers? Investors today tend to assess a proposition not only on the overall rate of return (broadly the actual cash yield likely to be earned by their investment from start to finish, discounted for time delays, and expressed in annual percentage terms) as balanced by the prospective risk, but also on the actual prospects of 'exit' (getting the cash investment back): there are very many short-term investors today whose sole motivation is to buy and sell quickly at a profit. Such exit today is no problem in a public company in which shares may be traded on the stock exchange, but is of critical importance in private companies. It would be going against the principles set out earlier for a corporation to be in any undue hurry to repay its venture capital, but what the model does provide is a built-in structure, and incentive, for the company to make arrangements at the appropriate time for the orderly repayment of the initial venture capital. Any private company, anxious to accumulate sufficient funds either to make proposals for the gradual repayment of its expensive risk capital (so as to free valuable equity units for the directors and workforce), or to gradually replace the initial risk capital by much cheaper, long-term loan investors for the same reason, must therefore be attractive to venture capital investors. There will still be a market, such as the Stock Exchange, for the resale of risk capital shares, but more importantly, for both public and private companies there will almost certainly be a *planned exit* for those shares.

Two points need to be emphasised here. Firstly, that a rate of interest is intended to be paid regularly on risk capital (and charged against profits before they are available to accumulate), so that the venture capital investor does get his basic cost of capital reimbursed. The second point is that it should be a practical proposition at some stage to re-accept the original risk capital on terms entitling the providers to fewer equity units (if not to start repaying the venture capital anyway), *before* all the accumulated reserves are actually paid out. Risk capital may cease to be risk capital after, say, five years, and the investor may see his capital begin to be repaid at that point, while he has throughout had a good rate of interest, yet, along with all the other contributories, he may still have to wait a further two or three years before he receives the real bonus profit deriving from the equity units. If this were not so, then it might take an inordinately long time for a corporation to reach maturity; the company needs to be able to either re-offer equity units, or else accumulate further reserves. Furthermore, all equity unit holders must be treated alike – and the investor gets a fair return on capital just as the other contributories receive a fair contractual payment, with a longer time horizon in relation to the bonus arising from equity participation.

To return for a moment to the stock market analysis referred to earlier, if the average FTSE 100 company (i.e., the average of the largest hundred companies on the London Stock Exchange) were to now be paying a regular cash dividend of say 15% per annum (net of basic rate tax and therefore still showing a substantial equity premium above market rates for equivalent bond issues) on its remaining original share capital, instead of an effective 48% per cent net, then out of the resulting savings it could repay the entirety of its share capital in annual instalments over a period of some three or four years. It could be suggested that this is misleading because it ignores the fact that the accumulated reserves *belong* to the share capital due to inflation and underpayments of dividend in the past. What do we say in response? We need to ask them what risk the investors feel they are taking *now* and in the years to come in relation to the amount of the original investment (in a company now worth several times the total original subscribed share capital) that justifies a *continuing* return of 48% per annum on it.

It is envisaged that a new division of the stock market would perform a vital role in providing access to five or ten year venture capital, not only for all corporations based on the new model, but also for smaller businesses. The present basis of distinction between public and private companies may need to be reconsidered for the new corporation, for which the more relevant distinction (for purposes of disclosure and monitoring) would seem to be sheer size or some other assessment of importance to the community, such as the number of equity unit holders. Some form of market for venture capital for all sizes of corporation must be an absolute necessity, although it would have some rather different features to the existing capital market. The criteria for choice of support for a share (apart from the obvious matters of the corporation's own standing and performance) would need to concentrate on the contractual, interim rate of return being offered, the number of equity units being offered with it, and the prospective date of repayment. If a clearer distinction were made between *real* risk capital, such as for start-ups, and other less vulnerable capital investment, such as continuation funding for established corporations, there would be a clearer route for capital seeking the highest potential rewards – which must be investment in new or smaller businesses, and of course those large businesses in high risk areas.

With regard to the technicalities of the issuing of share capital, this will be a matter of contractual bargaining between the directors and the capital providers in the same way as for the other contributories. An example might be as follows: capital to be invested for a fixed ten year term, repayable in annual instalments over the second half (years 6 to 10), and qualifying for a reasonably generous interim income return (perhaps around 10% or 15% per annum, paid at the end of each year), together with a significant slice of equity units until year 5 (enabling the possessor to share in the equity profits of the company). At that point the equity units held might be reduced in stages as repayment of the capital takes place. In some exceptional cases, the possession of equity units (and hence the sharing in equity profits) may actually continue beyond the date the risk capital was repaid. This is discussed in more detail in the next chapter.

There is no reason why such direct investment of capital in enterprise should not be highly profitable – the overall income return on risk capital (after taking into account the earnings from equity units as well) could end up nearer to 20, 30 or even 50% per annum, or even more in exceptional cases, commensurate with the risk – as it would be an uncertain return on genuine enterprise capital, as originally conceived in classical economics. Exactly how much it earns is up to the market.

In the care and control of punters

The trading of capital-related equity on stock exchanges is a sound concept and a proper exercise of market forces. What is questionable, however, is having the totality of a company's *ownership and control* so traded, because these features require the specific relationship of true participation. Shareholders are the wrong people to do this. How can proper participation, and the careful monitoring and control that is so desperately needed from equity holders, take place when shares are things acquired and disposed of with no concern other than for the gain to be made on them? How many shareholders turn up to a company's AGM to meet and quiz their directors? In the case of small shareholders, they tend to be genuinely disinterested. In the case of larger shareholders (other than institutions) they tend to be more interested in how much they can make from either a re-sale of the shares or the acquisition and restructuring of the company's assets (i.e., interfering in the company to seek private gain from it rather than being concerned for the interests of the company itself). Few public company shareholders have real concern for the interests of the company they invest in, or want to help see it prosper for its own sake.

It is beyond question that the operation of the free market as an economic mechanism (while it is not the answer to everything) can be extremely successful in the allocation of scarce resources in a commercial environment. Nevertheless it is vital that the ownership and control of corporations is vested in a body of participators more appropriate than existing shareholders. It is suggested that there are inherent faults in the structure of the conventional capitalist model, which not only generate extremes of inequality but also fail to achieve balanced and sustainable economic activity for the general benefit of the community.

It is argued that this is the case because, under the existing model, capital providers have become synonymous with short-term opportunistic punters who are encouraged by the stock market to follow a system of fast-entry, fast-exit and instant profit. By definition and by all mathematical models of their decision-making process, they only seek to maximise their immediate financial returns. There are today transactions in and then out of shares that take place, by computer program with no human supervision, in fractions of a second, and their frequency and scale will soon be (if they are not already) the great majority of all transactions in shares. Under our proposed new model, however, the vesting of equity control into the hands of all actively continuing contributories (especially management and workforce) is likely to provide the chance for a broader motivation: not just the seeking of an inexorable rise in earnings per share, but independence, sustainability and the general benefit to the community.

In the old company model, it has long been widely accepted that there is a strong element of shareholder apathy in larger, more well-established companies in particular. This led many years ago to the consequent loss of any real supervisory control and the complete absence of any structural monitoring of the board of directors, except perhaps in the financial press. Is that really acceptable, to have ultimate supervision of the operations and governance of our trade and industry to be in the hands of a few financial journalists and the occasional 'activist shareholder'? In the proposed model, and especially in the case of the well-established corporations, one reason why this is bound to be less likely is that the equity is in the hands, not so much of casual or temporary or remote investors, who in many cases expressly do not want to get involved (and who therefore simply 'cop out' by selling their shares at the first sign of trouble), but of those *expressly* involved in the corporation, and who can realistically be regarded as *participators* in it.

As corporations have become larger and larger, and transcended national boundaries, the sheer power exerted by a small board of directors over entities greater than some small nations, cries out for much more democratic control than can possibly be exercised by persons and institutions, whose sole declared collective interest is not the cohesive aim of satisfying the needs of the community, or even the best interests of the corporation, but the socially divisive aim of removing as much as possible from all other classes of contributory, so as to increase their own wealth as existing capital providers. It might not be such an inappropriate analogy to compare the present situation with the 'democracy' that formerly existed in the UK when the only voters enfranchised were those with sufficient freehold property to qualify. Why should capital ownership be a condition for participating in economic activity?

To give the matter a scientific analogy, and referring to the second law of thermodynamics, the existing capitalist world economy must be one of the few closed systems exhibiting symptoms of *reducing* entropy in terms of the relative wealth of the participants, and to that extent *must* be in a state of disequilibrium.

Those readers who appreciated this scientific analogy will also have noticed that the proposed corporate model is uniquely compatible with modern *'Gaia'* theory in environmental science: the corporation becomes self-regulatory, like the planet Earth, in the sense that its component structure (and therefore its nature or personality) adapts naturally and automatically to provide the ideal balance of contributories for the circumstances prevailing at any one time.

As a matter of interest, there are very many private and public charities in the UK that operate very successfully in a variety of fields of economic activity, yet have no shareholders at all. Here the target of financial independence (where it is possible) has usually been sought, and sometimes achieved, and the entity structured to some degree on the principles advocated in this book. It is revealing to consider how many of those organisations to which we all look for a contribution to basic human sustenance, medical aid, education, progress and harmony (and what economic activities could have more important aims?) are registered charities with no shareholders or owners at all.

Summary
This chapter on capital has been intentionally wide ranging, demonstrating that not only is capitalism a hindrance to successful business enterprise, as argued in previous chapters, it is also conceptually flawed. The focus of this chapter has been to demonstrate how the provision of capital is simply one contribution to the totality of corporate activity, and how the strategic importance of this contribution itself varies with time. Arguments have been marshalled which clearly show that the risk profile of venture capital changes with time, so that when a corporation is successful, its cost of capital should fall and not rise. This proposition is a crucial block in the foundation for the new model and it is argued to its conclusion. The dynamics of the proposed change are explored beyond the obvious, and it is demonstrated how the desired consequences of a high level of reinvestment, of employee participation, of director motivation and of price and cost flexibility all follow from the proposed structural changes. The importance of risk capital has been emphasised, and the likelihood of its more frequent recycling has been argued. Finally, the proposition that a framework for economic activity should be the object for casual ownership, as it is in the existing model, has been challenged.

5 The capital incentive problem

Introduction
One of the inescapable characteristics of a corporate model that seeks to reduce the dominance of capital is that, at the same time, we are bound to be reducing whatever advantages the feature of *capital incentive* is likely to have. This could represent a significant criticism of our proposed new model, and therefore needs to be confronted: let us be under no illusion that, for the businessman, the success of the model hinges on our being able to provide a conclusive response to this problem.

Firstly, let us set out precisely what the criticism is, and how far it ranges. Then we shall set about suggesting a number of possible ways of tackling the problem, finally providing the solution that, we argue, settles the issue completely.

The problem
Equity units are designed to fairly distribute to the participators the income arising from the economic activities of a corporation, and to provide the control of it in an effective way. What they do *not* automatically do – but what a traditional share does – is reward anyone for the *capital* value of a person's contribution. That is intentional, but the implications are profound. To fully understand the repercussions of this feature, let us examine a number of common examples where this might be relevant.

1. Firstly, we have an employee, possibly a director, who has been a key participator in a new and fast-growing corporation, such as an internet-related business. As a result of his contribution, he has bargained for, and been awarded, say 20% of the equity in that corporation. He helps to build up the business, and after a few

difficult years, it finally becomes very successful. He retires (or leaves for some other valid reason) after, say, ten years. During that ten years he has of course received not just his basic salary but also his 20% share of the corporate profits (his 'dividend' in traditional terms). Now, if the business had been a traditional capitalist corporation, he would in addition on retiring be able to sell his 20% stake in the company (i.e., his shares), which should provide him with a very welcome capital sum on top of it all. [Let us ignore the problems of selling private company shares.]

2. Secondly, we have an enterprising individual who takes on, say, empty premises in the high street, and spends several years building up a new business that is eventually quite successful. He took a significant risk in the early years, as the project could have failed; in the event he succeeded, and he now has a business with a substantial 'goodwill' value. The retail store is likely to produce good profits for some while to come, thanks to his commitment, effort, enterprise and risk. When he retires, he would like to 'sell' the business and reap the capital value of what he has done.

3. Finally, we have an employee in an established public company who has the capacity to make a lasting difference to it, i.e., with the benefits lasting beyond the present year. As an incentive, the directors want to provide him with what under the traditional model would be a share option: the opportunity to make a gain relating to the increase in *capital* value of the company during his employment.

These examples illustrate the problem that our proposed new model needs to accommodate. In short, it might be argued that any founder would have to be uniquely naïve or altruistic to consent to using the new model rather than the traditional model, as – on the face of it – he would have to part with the capital value of his business to either his staff or his successors, instead of enjoying the fruits himself. We shall respond that this is not the case. The specific argument that need to be rebutted here actually has two elements: firstly, that participators under the new model are unable to benefit from the *capital* value of their efforts, and secondly, that the physical cash payment for this would come (in the traditional model) from *outside* the company and so benefit the company at the cost only of outside investors. We need to establish that the new model settles the argument on *both* of these scores.

A preliminary response
It is accepted that equity units do not have any *capital* value. There are several reasons for this: (a) having a capital value would create an obstacle for those potential participators who would seek to acquire equity units but have no access to capital, (b) it defines the nature of participation universally in capital terms when this is the very feature we are trying to escape from, and (c) it provides the opportunity for others with capital (but no other interest in the company) to take over the business. More than anything, it offends the idea that a corporation is not an object for the casual ownership of those with wealth, but is a framework for economic activity in the community.

A response could therefore be that it is simply greedy for entrepreneurs and key participators to expect even more than a good salary and a share in annual profits. Many individuals would be perfectly content with that; indeed many of those employees with no prospect of participation in the traditional model would relish the idea of participation in the new model. But that is not a good enough response. The case has been made that those who have held equity units for some time and who (such as in the examples quoted above) have participated in creating a corporation or making it a success, need to derive some *additional* benefit (broadly equivalent to a capital gain under the traditional model) from their efforts.

There could be a special category of equity units such as 'founder's shares'. These could be limited to a portion of the equity and would carry a capital value, i.e., they could be traded. This would introduce capital from outside the company to pay a reward to the key players within the company. These equity units would be indistinguishable from existing traditional shares, available to public investors. The drawback to some equity units being saleable on the open market is that the holders would almost certainly sell them, just as most small investors in privatised utilities couldn't wait to cash in their holdings, with the result that the company would end up exactly like the traditional company, with outside 'capital' shareholders. And if the equity units were not saleable, then with no 'exit', they wouldn't be worth much at all. They could be redeemable by the company itself: but that would take years and would drain the company of resources. It is therefore concluded that such a hybrid solution is unsatisfactory.

Another possibility is to account internally for variations in the value of the company's goodwill. Now, the standard Income Statement (suitably amended to show it in value added terms) and the standard Balance Sheet can be made to articulate, simply because they are fundamentally based on double-entry bookkeeping. In other words, a profit of £10 shows up at the same time in the balance sheet as precisely £10 in extra net assets (whether as extra stock, debtors or cash at bank). Therefore the precise net surplus each year also gets to be the figure added to the amount due to be distributed to equity unit holders. So far so good. But the amount needed to recognise the growth in value of the company over the year is not just the increase in net assets (i.e., the trading surplus) but also the increase in value of the *goodwill* of the company. When this 'goodwill' is added to the net assets, then the company balance sheet broadly shows what the company is worth, i.e., what it could be sold for in its entirety in the traditional way. So if we were to get the auditors to estimate the value of the goodwill each year (awkward but not impossible), then the increase or decrease over the year could be included with the profit as the amount ultimately payable to equity unit holders. This need only be done in those companies for which it is a significant issue and where the equity holders so choose.

There are several objections to this suggestion. Firstly, a goodwill increase does not represent any value added to the market. It creates nothing for the community, so the company would be paying cash out and rewarding people for no underlying increase in economic wealth. The cost would come from within the company too, rather than from external investors. Secondly, the concept of *goodwill* as an asset is incompatible with our concept of the new corporation as a framework for economic activity in the community; a massive goodwill value may well in fact reflect that there is insufficient competition (too great a monopoly), or that the business is charging too much to its captive community, which is transferring excessive resources to the beneficiaries holding equity units.

Both the above solutions represent an abandonment of the ideals of the new model. Something rather better is required.

A more thorough analysis

When equity units are issued, the terms of the issue are agreed at the start. It would be relatively easy to include some additional provision such that the possessor of certain of those units could, once they have been owned for a specific number of years, have their ownership extended for (say) an additional three or five, or even ten years *beyond* the date at which they would normally become inactive. For example, when a key long-term participator retires, she may still be able to receive her 'dividend' share of profits for a further number of years after she had left.

Such a proposal for post-active payments would encourage participators to stay for the longer term, and reward them by in effect giving their equity share a significant additional value, equivalent perhaps to the capital value of a traditional share. The cost would be borne by the remaining equity unit holders in the company that had received the benefit of their contribution, which is logical: the later equity holders (who would be enjoying the advantage of the earlier contributions) would simply bear some of the cost of rewarding those earlier ones. There would, however, be no permanent burden on the company, and the company would not be paying out cash and rewarding people without any increase in economic wealth. The post-active payments are only being made because the equity holder created them. Moreover, the company would not be vulnerable to complete outsiders taking it over by buying up its shares.

An important point to be made is that a corporation is what the key participators – indeed all the participators – make it. So when one of them leaves, for example, the corporation's remaining value depends on the contributions of those remaining, and the circumstances now obtaining. Nothing, least of all a business, has any *permanent* value, as circumstances affecting that value, and the individuals creating it, are changing all the time. The capital value, such as of a share, is illusory. It is an artificial construct reflecting that a certain set of circumstances obtaining at present is likely to produce an anticipated level of income in the future. If those circumstances change, and they always do, as nothing is permanently unchanging, then the anticipated income will vary.

Obviously traditional shares, being indirect ownership of underlying real assets, are, in an inflationary environment, likely to see growth regardless of their management, but that has little to do with participation in the true creation of wealth – or economic activity that actually adds anything to the market. It does not put more products or more services into more people's hands. It increases the extremes of inequality by simply adding to those with existing wealth, and it does this in a way that does not reward enterprise so much as mere wealth possession.

It is important to appreciate that, although the 'value' of a share seems to be paid by the market outside the corporation, nevertheless this is always only in the interim period. Ultimately, the full benefit of a share has to come entirely from within the company in terms of what it actually earns for its possessor. There may be an interim valuation by the outside market – and that market may well pay an interim price for the share, based on that valuation (thus providing an early opportunity of 'exit') – but ultimately the sole source of any value at all, any earnings whatsoever, comes directly and exclusively from the company of which the share is a part. It is the actual earnings (plus perhaps a tiny element of liquidation value) of the share that generates any worth it may have. Without the prospect of earnings or break-up value from its own company, a share is worthless, whatever the market may *provisionally* think of it in the meantime. Hence we are *not* wrong to see the future earnings of the corporation as the sole source of the value of its equity. And moreover, we have established that the capital reward to an investor does not actually come from the market *outside* the company, except on a provisional or interim basis: ultimately it can only come from within the company itself.

The problem we have with a traditional share is that it purports to give you a right to a share in the earnings of the company *for the rest of the company's existence.* This is the nub of the issue here. You even get this infinite flow of dividends if you sell the share, only then it's effectively discounted to the present day and paid on exit (by someone else in the market). By contrast, equity units under our proposed new model offer you an appropriate share of current income plus perhaps *five or ten years of future income*, paid eventually. So the 'capital incentive' of an equity unit would always be rather less than the capital incentive of a traditional share.

But let's think really carefully about this. What exactly *is* the value of an individual's contribution to the economic activity of a corporation? Let's identify it and value it precisely: it is the additional net surplus arising or anticipated to arise as a result of that contribution. And what is the closest approximation that we can make to this figure? It is the additional surplus that arises in the current year and possibly in the next few years to come. The benefit to the company may well last for the foreseeable future (i.e., five to ten years), but is rather unlikely to last to the end of the company's life. After all, others will be making further and better contributions later in the company's life. Now, in our proposed model, this benefit is precisely what the individual will receive her share in: the current surplus, plus her share in the surplus for the next few years. Compare this, however, with the incentive of an allocation of shares. What benefit do these shares bring? They bring the possessor a share in the profits for the current year, plus the profits for the foreseeable future – and then the profits for evermore to the end of the company's life. Now, let's be absolutely honest: which is the more appropriate reward?

Does a contribution to a company in this period really deserve a share in *all the income* that that company produces in future periods for evermore? What has that shareholder done that deserves a share in the income arising in fifty years' time? Is not some, or most, of that later income attributable to the efforts of all those other successors contributing afterwards? To suggest that additional fresh shares (diluting the existing equity) can always be issued later for further contributions is not the point, as the existing shares are still there demanding a dividend, demanding their continuing share from the later efforts of the corporation. The proposed new model regards it as appropriate that a contribution today deserves what it produces in the current year, plus perhaps (if the contribution is a reasonably lasting one) for the foreseeable future (i.e., the next five to ten years). The circumstances in business and industry change materially over a ten-year period, and depend on what inputs take place throughout that period.

Our response to the problem of 'capital incentive' really is quite simple: if an individual's contribution is likely to have value to the company beyond the current year's trading, then that contribution deserves an extension of the period for which the individual gets benefit from his equity units – the precise period depending solely on an estimate of the likely period for which the benefit is expected. And the amount of the benefit is exactly what actually arises over that subsequent term. The incentive could not be more tailor-made.

So let's now look again at the three examples set out at the start of this chapter, which formed the criticism of our proposed new model, and see if our response is able to provide the incentive that we found was necessary in each of those examples:

Firstly, the key participator with a 20% interest in the company. On retiring, he will probably receive ten years of further income from his 'investment', after he retires, in addition to what he has already received. This surely exhausts the value of his input; he is no longer actively contributing to the company, and after ten years, a fast-moving company will almost certainly depend on others for its profits. If there were a genuine *capital* value in his original contribution to the company, then perhaps his company should have paid him a capital sum to acquire it from him. In any other circumstances, it is difficult to see how he could justify a permanent stake. If his contribution included the provision of a small amount of risk capital at the start of the enterprise, then this is presumably now being repaid to him; the fact that the company can repay this (or easily replace it) must indicate that it is no longer capital *at risk* and accordingly its provision today would no longer attract 20% of the equity: he therefore could no longer justify holding on to 20% of the equity once the value of any other contribution has ceased. Giving him traditional shares would therefore have been an excessive reward, as these would be valued as if the benefits of his ten-year contribution were everlasting.

Secondly, the founder of a company who sets up a new retail business. In view of the very substantial contribution that he made – without which there would be no corporation – he could well justify a lengthy post-active period, possibly even 15 or 20 years. This would only be limited by market pressure from other equity holders and the directors: it is entirely up to them. But, again, how would you justify his deserving *a lifetime* of income payments (i.e., the equivalent of being paid for the totality of his shares)? Surely after five or ten or fifteen years beyond the date he retires, the retail store will have needed many more contributions to its management and direction to ensure that it still competes and produces a surplus. Do those individuals not deserve some equity reward? To award the founder with the value of the entire company at the date he retires (i.e., letting him sell his shares, or indeed even to keep them) means that his contribution in founding it was equal to the total prospective earnings of the business in the future, for evermore. That is a ludicrous proposition: it presumes that no further input would ever be needed.

We then come to example number three: an employee who, today, raises the *capital* value of the company by her actions, and wants to see a fair and reasonable portion of that increase. Again, it is hard to see that the increase in value will be permanently everlasting, justifying a *lifetime* of income from this action, but there is a case to be made that she deserves the award of five or ten years' worth of the extra income, on top of her existing salary plus profit share.

The solution in all these cases has to be post-active participation in earnings. One impact of this is that it restricts what is left for the subsequent equity holders, but then they owe as much to those who've gone before them. If a person's contribution has increased profits by a certain amount, reducing over the next few years, then that person deserves to share in that extra amount. There is, however, no logic in rewarding someone for key work in the early stages by giving them (part) ownership of the enterprise for evermore. That is where the capital-based corporation goes wrong. It excessively rewards the early (capital) investors; the market then rewards successive investors; and this in turn forces the company to squeeze all its other participators (the employees, the suppliers, and the customers) more and more in order to maintain the servicing it needs to make to the current investors. The outcome is the inevitably increasing gross inequality in wealth.

It is more appropriate to reward with current income plus the next few years of income, where this has been earned (i.e., where it is directly enhanced by the value of a person's contribution), without giving them the value of those who contribute subsequently in all the years to come. In this sense, traditional shares bring too early a reward to those earliest in the chain: the stock market constantly rewards *current* shareholders on the basis of *future* anticipated earnings (and on the assumption that these last forever), rather than on what has been achieved today. What a participator has earned is, by contrast, this year's profit plus (in appropriate circumstances) that of the next few years – but only *when* they happen, and *if* they do, and then it's precisely *that profit*, not the outside market's perception, viewed from today, of what those future years might have brought. So our proposed scheme does offer the equivalent of a 'capital incentive' but discounts this with a dose of reality. Your contribution may turn out to be short-term, or affected by other future events or circumstances: post-active equity units reflect that, while traditional shares do not.

One further observation we could make concerns the related issue of 'goodwill', touched on in the second example discussed above. The 'capital' value of a traditional share is somewhat similar to the 'capital' value of the accounting concept of 'goodwill': they are both an estimate of the capitalized value of future earnings. When an unincorporated business is sold, its valuation is based partly on the net assets of that business, and partly on the goodwill value. A property rental business is valued almost entirely on the basis of its net assets, whereas a professional firm for example, has few assets but a lot of goodwill; the same goes for a traditional 'CTN' newsagents or almost any high street retail store. If you subsequently examine the trading of a business whose value consists largely of real assets, those assets will obviously have been transferred. But if you ask a businessman whether purchased *goodwill* has had its full value transferred, he will invariably respond that *it depends on the buyer*: in other words, it's largely a matter of what the buyer makes of it, or how well he compares to the vendor, or how well he fits the role he has taken over. That of course is precisely what we are arguing about with regard to the value of shares, that they cannot properly be valued solely by extrapolating the past, they do depend on the contribution of future participators. In other words, today's capital value of a traditional share does actually *depend* on future contributors to the company, so why do we allow shareholders to own all the future income as if that all belongs to the person who gave a contribution in the past?

Conclusion

The equity unit model has a perfectly satisfactory means of rewarding and incentivising the key participants in economic activity, by means of post-active payments. The reward is arguably more accurate and more suitable than that of share incentives. Our response to the problem of 'capital incentive' really is quite simple: if an individual's contribution is likely to have value to the company beyond the current year's trading, then that contribution deserves an extension of the period for which the individual gets benefit from his equity units – the precise period depending solely on an estimate of the likely period for which the benefit is expected. And the amount of the benefit is exactly what arises over that subsequent term. The incentive could not be more tailor-made.

Under our proposal, the participator receives a reward calculated to be precisely equal to his contribution. The traditional share, by contrast, carries an assertion of permanence that is illusory. It is illusory because a business has to dynamically adapt to circumstances, just like everything else in life, and in the same way, no one's contribution has permanent value. The corporation constantly moves on and the contribution of each participator tends to fade after a few years as new participators come in and move the corporation forward in a slightly different direction.

We can now respond to the criticism raised at the start of this chapter – that it would be regarded as naïve or altruistic for an entrepreneur to start off a new business under the new model rather than within the traditional corporation, as his reward would be unable to benefit from the capital value of his efforts, and the reward would not come from the outside market. The response to this criticism would be *NO* on all counts. The entrepreneur would more likely be regarded as enlightened, because

- there would be greater opportunity to involve others as and when this became necessary (and to do so without *permanently* committing the equity), thus increasing the prospects of growth;

- capital rewards do not in fact come from the market outside the corporation, except on a provisional, interim basis – ultimately they can only ever come from within the company;

- the entrepreneur would still be able to receive a very generous and appropriate reward for his efforts; indeed, instead of being altruistic, he is only parting with some of the equity to others if those others are likely to increase the value of that equity by an equivalent amount; and

- he would have a more harmonious and successful corporation overall.

A change in the attitude to the ownership of economic activity is necessary to bring economics up to date, just like a fresh attitude was once needed to the ownership of slaves. Those individuals contributing to the economic improvement of human society should be rewarded by such economic activity. The mere possession of special skills or talent may be arbitrary, but the exercise of them for the benefit of society does merit reward. Similarly, the mere possession of capital wealth may be arbitrary: it should not be the *ownership* of wealth that deserves reward, so much as its exercise or application in the creation of economic activity for the benefit of all.

The driving force behind business economics – and what the structure of the corporation requires – is that it should generate more wealth for society, that it should share it among those producing it, and do so fairly and justly, so that it improves the economic circumstances of all those involved in it. If the profit motive works for shareholders, surely it works just as well for all the other participators? The existing framework of the corporation has exactly the wrong effect: it squeezes what it can from all the participators in order to add to the stock of wealth solely of the owner of capital. The *employment of capital* in business enterprise deserves reward because it helps to produce something – it helps to add value to the market. The *ownership of business* by contrast simply stifles enterprise because it corners the results of that enterprise. It takes the profits from those who have produced it and gives it to those simply in possession of capital. This inevitably results in an inexorably rising inequality that adds no value to the market: society overall is no better off.

The capital-based corporation is as outdated an economic model as the idea of owning slaves, or of having a colonial empire. It is concerned with the benefits of an activity solely and exclusively for a single participator – the party with capital or power – rather than the overall interests of the human community as a whole.

It is time to replace it.

6 Corporate governance

Effective control by equity holders: a new philosophy
The directors *direct* the corporation, but it is the equity unit holders who ultimately *control* it. Because they represent all the persons with particular interest in the affairs of the corporation, including of course the directors themselves, the equity unit holders as a body are ideally placed to exercise such control. They are likely to have a slightly different and broader – and possibly more composite – perspective than the directors. The arrangements for exercising this control are what concern corporate governance.

In view of the old-established procedures for governance in the present UK model of the limited company, one could suggest that the equity unit holders should meet at least once a year at an Annual General Meeting (AGM), and that it should be here that they exercise their control. But we do not have to follow what has been done in the past with the traditional model – our task in this book is to devise what is most appropriate to our new model. And that is why we must ask whether it really is adequate for effective control to be exercised over any type of corporation (even if not particularly large or complex) in a single meeting once a year.

To answer this question, let us look briefly at a couple of examples drawn from opposite ends of the spectrum: a small, new corporation and a large, well established one, and consider what conclusion we might reach from this for corporations in general.

Let us imagine that you are a contributor to a small, new, high technology corporation, and that you have appointed me as one of your directors. You have perhaps invested a significant amount of your personal savings, or contributed significantly in some other way, but certainly enough to justify a material holding of equity units, although you are not in a position for one reason or another to actually be a director of the corporation yourself. You appreciate that this is going to be a high-risk venture, and no one really knows how things will develop. Do you really expect to wait more than twelve months (and possibly up to eighteen months) before you hear from me with the first reports on how things are going? Do you expect to rely on nothing more than anecdotal snippets of gossip to comfort you that your investment is safe and sound? Would you then honestly be content with a formal two or three hour meeting once a year? Or would you expect that, even though you may not be a director (and therefore not involved on a day-to-day basis, as you probably have your own full-time commitment elsewhere), you nevertheless ought to have, by prior agreement and without any special concession which might be withdrawn, brief monthly contact, with some sort of basic information on the performance of the business, the latest position on production/sales, and its updated prospects?

It is difficult to see how any company can argue against a brief monthly meeting, even if it is in the evening or sometimes in an informal setting, as being the cost of satisfying those people who have enabled the company to exist. We manage to achieve this when we run the local village hall! The pattern could become established with this meeting being the second part of a monthly board meeting of the directors. No expensive, detailed accounts need to be produced, but the directors would report – perhaps in a shortened version of what they reported ten minutes earlier to the directors' meeting – on all the usual strategic matters (possibly excluding detail on specifically contentious confidential items) and perhaps answer a few queries. In companies of all sizes, such a regular monthly forum would tend to promote a greater sense of involvement and participation, and achieve closer acquaintance between unit holders and the directors than could ever be the case with the existing over-formalised soulless and confrontational AGM format. The directors would probably appreciate the input of such 'governors', especially if they had a different background, as they might then have much to contribute and be a 'sounding board' for some of the directors' ideas.

Now let us consider a large, well-established corporation. It has often been said that the economic power of large corporations is greater than that of many small nations. That is perfectly true. The market value of the top 100 UK companies (those in the FTSE 100 index) was, in October 2014 (when this paragraph was first written), the sum of £1,750 billion. The precise amount on the day it was checked came to £1,749,912,850,000 – a *huge* amount of economic power by any standard. While a company's market value does not in itself mean a lot in terms of functional resources, it does give some idea of the enormous influence that the half-dozen or so principal directors of each of these hundred large companies have on the individual lives and families of the many millions affected by them. Can this really be effectively supervised by the owners of all this wealth in a two- or three-hour meeting, once a year?

You might wonder how we would feel if Parliament were only allowed to meet for one afternoon a year, for a single period of debate, with no organised opposition parties, no other opportunity for concerted opposition, and no forum for those voting to meet each other (prior to voting) for informed discussion. The minuscule accountability of large corporations to their contributors is the poorest testament to capitalist democracy: indeed, the large UK corporation could fairly be said to be literally a one-party state. The contestability of corporate bosses (by hostile take-over rather than by formal challenge at the AGM itself) is hailed by some commentators as the preferred weapon of supervision: hardly different from the contestability of dictators by a military coup. Is that to be the proud end-product of all the corporate governance and stewardship regulation?

Perhaps we should consider the possibility of unit holders electing a committee of their number, once this number exceeds a manageable amount. Such a committee – let us call them governors – would have no function whatever other than to represent the interests of the equity holders who elect them. This concept has already been referred to earlier in this book. In theory, these persons need not be equity holders as such themselves, provided that they were appointed by the equity holders to be their effective representatives. Such a body of half a dozen or so governors could be the ones to meet the directors monthly, acting almost like a 'shadow cabinet'. Indeed, the resources of large public corporations could probably extend to paying these governors a modest amount for their time so that, being truly independent (as their only masters are the unit holders who appoint them), they would replace the function presently carried out by non-executive directors. It is suggested that governors would be more effective than non-executive directors, simply because (a) their role is much more clearly defined without any inherent conflict, (b) they are not selected by, appointed by or answerable to, the directors, and (c) they have *legitimate authority* to monitor, discipline and control the board of directors: they are the owners, it is *their* company. They do in fact almost embody the best features of a non-executive chairman at the same time. This committee would be the obvious body to select, appoint and pay the auditors; and it could make its own comments to the main body of unit holders at the AGM.

It is therefore suggested that, for all corporations, there should be a pattern of brief monthly sessions to which either all equity unit holders, or at least a committee of them, are invited and a forum provided for discussion on the corporation's affairs. The philosophy for this type of control does, however, need to be very different from the entirely nominal and rather lifeless involvement of shareholders in a limited company. Unit holders are intended to be an integral part of the whole strategic process of governing and directing the corporation, because they are, and want to be, involved in it.

The Annual General Meeting (AGM)

We now return to the major event to which all unit holders are invited without exception, namely the Annual General Meeting or AGM. The concept of the AGM is enshrined in the western world's way of life just as much as the concept of the twelve-month accounting period. It has become optional for private companies since October 2007, but otherwise is probably here to stay.

> "The annual general farce: what is the point of companies' annual meetings? In America and Britain big shareholders rarely bother to attend, leaving small investors to eat a free lunch with top managers. In Germany big shareholders put in an appearance at the lengthy meetings, but little that is controversial is said. In France meetings are brief and poorly attended, even though some firms pay shareholders a small fee if they turn up."
>
> *(The Economist, 12th March 1994)*

Such an observation is commonplace. Under the present model, investors simply aren't interested, or equipped, to carry out a supervisory role as owner, and the cards are stacked against them if they try. This illustrates the utter fallacy of equating ownership and control with the risk capital provision: the two are quite separate functions.

It is suggested that an AGM of the *real* participators in a corporation is likely to be a more popular and meaningful forum, simply because the affairs of the corporation are bound to be far more relevant to these people.

What form of AGM do we envisage may be relevant to the proposed model of the corporation? The meeting needs to receive and consider a report by the directors on how well the corporation has performed under the control and governorship of the directors and unit holders together as a composite body. This does not mean just monitoring growth or profitability or earnings per share: it means assessing how far the company has gone in achieving whatever goals were set at the previous AGM for its economic activity to achieve – and this could encompass improving quality, reducing staff turnover, increasing productivity, keeping prices competitive, even reducing the corporation's environmental footprint – as well as the more traditional tests.

Those who have provided a contribution to the company must have some means of examining the result; and this result will reflect not only the performance of the directors, but of the teamwork of all those participators within the corporation. The chairman of the AGM might usefully be selected from the unit holder governors, rather than being the chairman of the directors: that would more readily match the true concept of what the AGM is supposed to be. The centre-piece of the first part of the AGM must be the objective report by the auditors (see Chapter 7), who were the persons chosen by the contributors the previous year, and paid by them, to compile the independent report on the year's results. This provides the figures for financial performance; it is then for the directors to present their own report adding flesh to the bones of the figures and possibly explaining the variations from the budget agreed the previous year. Everybody present would then have the opportunity to question both the directors and the auditors.

Another component of the AGM should concern the future more than the past: the presentation by the directors (possibly after prior publication and consultation with governors) of their plans for the coming year, and possibly for the next few years, upon which the corporation's performance will be judged at the following AGM.

Among the novel features in this business plan will need to be the proposed number of equity units to be issued over the next year (this needs to be determined so that, in future bargaining, it is known what value each unit is likely to have in the context of the whole) and the likelihood of there being any cash surplus for redeeming and cancelling passive equity units.

The publication of some sort of budget or forecast is an important part of the AGM. If a bank lends money, even on full security, the manager will generally argue that she needs to see a budget or cash flow forecast to satisfy herself that the company can adequately service its liabilities; on that basis it is illogical that those providing some additional contribution *without* security should be supplied with anything less. The argument for commercial confidence is remarkably weak in this respect, and largely disappears when everybody has to provide the same type of information. In any event, it remains unproven that confidentiality is actually beneficial. Secrecy is deeply and obsessively ingrained in all forms of commercial enterprises, but one wonders whether sometimes it is counter-productive. Its effect is to deliberately exclude those who would like to think that they participate within the corporation; and confidentiality is routinely and unthinkingly assumed to be the most suitable default approach.

A lot of the information provided by the historical accounts is at present used by investors, lenders, suppliers and workforce pay negotiators to enable them to make some sort of estimate of the forecast for the current year. So if that's the end product, why don't the directors publish their own forecast in the first place, so that we all get it right and avoid a lot of effort and guesswork? It makes sense to include some brief forecast as primary information prepared by those most able to control the events and variables in practice, i.e., the management. It could be said that comparability of different firms' forecasts might be suspect, and that degrees of optimism will not be uniform; but lack of absolute objectivity is a poor reason for denying the information altogether. In any event, after the first year there will be a public record of management's consistency in achieving its set targets. In some trades – and in some economic times – reliable forecasting is virtually impossible: it will be a worthwhile exercise for this point to be made.

Any such forecast should be accompanied by sufficient notes to identify the assumptions which have been made in compiling it, and to explain how ambitious, or how cautious, the forecast is, and it might even illustrate how potential variances in performance are likely to affect the financial position by next year. Major capital movements also need to be included. The forecast is a test of the professionalism of the directors in the context of the overall economy, and should embody whatever policies the equity holders may have laid down.

If the directors are to be seen to be ultimately controlled by the equity unit holders – which is the whole idea of this proposal – then they should be prohibited from having any remuneration or benefit of any kind as directors, until the AGM has openly and expressly considered the matter and voted on it. Of course the directors can lay down their terms as they think fit: outstanding directors are immensely valuable and they are going to know it. But the whole remuneration package for the coming year – including the allocation of any equity units (and it would seem vital that the directors participate significantly) – must be the subject of an express vote each year (or perhaps each three years) at an AGM along with the re-appointment of the director.

The practical ability of the equity unit holders to appoint and dismiss any or all of the directors, and to decide precisely on their remuneration, and to select and appoint the auditors and decide precisely on their remuneration, is absolutely critical to avoid *de facto* control of the corporation falling to the existing board of directors and (sometimes) a minority core of active equity holders. This is known to happen in many existing public limited companies in the UK and elsewhere at the present time. The concentration of the unit holders' power into the hands of an executive or governing committee, composed, we would hope, of individuals as effective, dedicated and competent as the directors themselves, will go a long way to ensuring more balanced control in such circumstances.

To the AGM needs to be invited every existing equity unit holder (whether active or passive) as they are the persons who have a clear and accepted stake in the company, although as the control is expressly in the hands of active equity unit holders only, these latter are the only ones logically able to vote on a resolution.

Democratic expression
Again, the authority to be exercised by the equity unit holders requires that the appointment of any new additional director could

only be made after discussion at a monthly unit holders' meeting. They may possibly even want to meet him in an informal interview – that is, after all, the absolute reality of what is supposed to be taking place even in the traditional model!

The need for the contributors to a corporation to be able to commit the directors to applying funds in a specific way was originally built into the present UK model by means of the 'objects clause' of the Memorandum of Association. This specified the objects for which the company had been formed, and the company was deemed not to have the power to engage in incompatible activities. Unfortunately, the practical effect of this restriction was that other parties, contracting with the company in good faith on what they had reasonably considered to be perfectly legitimate activities, could, and did, end up not being paid for their claims. This doctrine, known as the *ultra vires* doctrine, was swept away by the European Communities Act of 1972, and since then there has been no equivalent practical way of restricting the directors' activities to what the investors wanted. This itself represents a sound legal argument for the directors to have to commit themselves more clearly to their proposed activities for the advance agreement of the other contributories.

What does it mean if the directors part with even just *one per cent* of the equity to a contributor? The moment they accept the equity participation of any other contributor than themselves, they are saying that they will *involve* that other person – by providing information, in consultation, and in strategic decision making. They do not have to agree with her all the time, but they must involve her and pay due regard to her interests. The unit holders *must* be involved in the corporation.

How should decisions be reached at a general meeting of unit holders? The consensus at the present time for most meetings of all sorts of groups, is that, after presentation of the facts, answering of questions, and general discussion, a vote should be taken. [It is a fundamental presumption of democracy that not only is the stated opinion of any one voter, equal in quality and merit to that of any other, but also that the best interests of the group are equal to the opinions expressed by the greatest number of those voicing them.] This vote could be a simple vote of those present, one per person, as in a show of hands, but an arguably more accurate vote is one in which each vote is weighted according to the number of units held, and specific postal ('proxy') votes are counted as well, although this obviously can only apply to those resolutions already listed on the agenda for the meeting. A secret ballot is not normally considered necessary for company business.

A simple majority, i.e., more than half the votes cast, may be a suitable test for general issues, but for really strategic decisions it seems wrong to proceed with a policy when nearly half the unit holders may disagree. If we were to include those not casting a vote, it is possible that more than half had not specifically consented to a particular course of action. The present UK rules take this into account by providing that certain strategic decisions require the approval of 75 per cent of those voting (as weighted by the number of shares held) to be obtained, after proper prior notice of the particular resolution had been sent to all members, offering them the ability to cast a postal vote as well. There are also extensive statutory rules intended to protect the interests of minorities, whenever these might be unfairly prejudiced or oppressed.

All these rules have been carefully thought out, having been built up over a long period of practical experience with the problems of commercial trading, and it is envisaged that a similar body of rules will need to apply to the conduct of the proposed corporate model, for precisely the same reasons.

As has been stated before, the proposed model is sufficiently flexible in that it caters for the possibility of the very tightly controlled enterprise in which the directors provide virtually all of the equity contribution of every description; in such a case, the directors are free to exercise complete control (subject to statutory controls over disclosures at the AGM and the national registration office) and to reap the entirety of the rewards. No-one would begrudge them that in those circumstances. But as soon as other persons are needed to produce the rewards, then market pressures are likely to ensure that those rewards are shared. As soon as there are any permanent employees whose contribution is material to the corporation's success, then it makes practical business sense for these employees to be represented among the unit holders. As the business grows, so it usually becomes more and more dependent upon other contributories such as the employees, and they accordingly acquire a greater share in the control of the undertaking and in the fruits of its success. It is envisaged that a mature corporation will be largely controlled by the directors and workforce jointly, although many capital-intensive corporations will always have a high level of equity involvement by the capital-providers.

All this has been stated before. But the point is, once the directors have parted with any proportion of the equity, even if only in a lot of small parcels, then they will be forced to consult with and listen to the equity unit holders, who become their bosses in a very real way. The existing practice of enabling equity voters to give a *general* power of proxy to the chairman of a meeting of shareholders (where this person is also the chairman of the board of directors, as happens in the present company model), is really a defeat of the democratic process which the AGM is supposed to represent. In a parliamentary election, we would not tolerate the outgoing prime minister having sacks full of blank proxy votes to cast as he thought fit! If an equity holder cannot be troubled to turn up and vote, then he must abstain, or send in his specific vote on agenda issues, or ask a specific representative of himself to attend and vote in his place. The equity unit holders as a body are the ultimate supervisors of the directors. They can always abstain if they do not hold strong views; but if they wield *ultimate* control, then they cannot logically assign or *delegate* ultimate decisions.

Committee of governors

Reference was made earlier to the appointment of a committee of unit holders or participators once the number of such contributories became unwieldy. There are arguments for and against this. The principal disadvantage is the way in which the democratic process is then diluted by being left to a handful of active members who may be unrepresentative in attitude – although these representatives will of course always have been elected by the majority. The advantage, however, is that such a small committee would be far more effective by being referred to more frequently than once a year, perhaps more informally, and could meet with the directors (perhaps in confidence) once a month to monitor and control the enterprise, having in such circumstances access to regular management figures and being privy to the strategic decisions normally made only by the directors – all as discussed earlier in this chapter – and they would be the appropriate council to select, appoint and pay the auditors, and to interview proposed new directors. There is some merit in the suggestion that all but the most minor of companies should have such a committee, and that at least one member should represent each of the principal classes of contributory, so as to be fully representative. It is even arguable, for rather larger companies, that a representative of the consumers, or of the wider economic environment, might be appointed to such a committee to give an element of external balance.

How should such a committee be appointed? They are, in effect, almost a 'shadow cabinet', a shadow board of directors, and should therefore be selected and appointed in much the same way. It would seem appropriate that they should put their names forward, supported by a number of sponsors from among the unit holders, with a brief 'manifesto', to then be elected by normal ballot of the equity unit holders.

It should be pointed out that the word 'committee' has been used throughout this book, simply because people know what a committee is, although it is acknowledged that this term does have somewhat dreary and negative connotations. Yet a board of directors is as much a committee as that of unit holders. The word committee has been chosen because it is then clear that this is a body elected democratically by and out of unit holders so as to represent them: the hope, however, is that the body so elected becomes more of a team having the positive direction and vision which has always been associated with free market enterprise economics. The whole system of directors and governors should work together as one with, largely, a mutuality of aims: individual personalities are an important part of this, and the proposed system should be seen more as providing a broader base of strong and supportive organisational resource than as a mechanically clattering administration.

The prospect of loss

A detailed discussion on the impact of trading losses takes place later in this book in chapter 10, but for our present purposes we need to consider the governance of a corporation which has incurred such a level of losses that it faces the prospect of insolvency, i.e., not being able to pay all its debts in full. The ordinary purpose of corporate governance concerns the control of a corporation for the benefit of its contributors. Once insolvency is in prospect, the interest in the corporation of those existing contributories becomes nil – or even negative, if they are responsible for bearing losses. Clearly this has profound repercussions. Those who, up to now, have had the control of the corporation, must have exercised it in such a way that losses have been incurred and their equity interest has become eliminated. Their responsibility (if any) will be considered in chapter 10, but for the moment our concern must be that control of the corporation must be able to pass to such persons who have a continuing economic interest in it.

At the first prospect of insolvency, the directors or the unit holders must call a meeting of all equity unit holders. The date of this meeting must constitute the end of the current accounting period, so that an account can, if required, subsequently be drawn in order to allocate the losses to the respective unit holders up to that date. It also constitutes the start of a fresh accounting period if it is resolved that the corporation should continue to trade. At that meeting a decision needs to be made as to whether the corporation ceases to trade and winds up, or whether it should carry on. Clearly it can only carry on if this is likely to be beneficial to all the contributories involved. A new plan will need to be proposed, accompanied by additional capital, or an offer of deferred payment terms by suppliers, or possibly a reduction in suppliers' prices or employees' wages. Directors may have to change and/or accept reduced salaries along with everybody else. A workable plan with an adequate margin for contingencies may be possible. In that event, insolvency becomes effectively the death of the old corporation and the instant rebirth of a new one, achieved by a simple but bold adjustment of internal costs and a thorough shuffling of the equity units – and, of course, the control.

Often the contributories to a corporation (or to a limited company in present circumstances) would prefer to continue trading rather than to see the corporation collapse and disappear. They may prefer to take somewhat lower returns or wages if the alternative is nothing at all. To have a rigid definition of insolvency 'in order to protect creditors' can be counter-productive. The costs of a winding up are in practice so high, and the procedure takes so long, that creditors tend to lose out badly. What the contributories – and the creditors – most need, apart from confidence in the directors being able to adhere to a workable plan, is confidence that a fair balance will be maintained between all of them. A proposal that all suppliers holding equity units give one extra month's credit, all employees (with equity units) take a 5 per cent wage cut and all capital providers find another few per cent of capital, might well resuscitate a dying company and be sufficient contribution by those previously responsible for it, to satisfy the external unsecured creditors (who would otherwise lose out) that they should wait for a few months before demanding payment of arrears. In the context of the proposed model, such a plan can be put into practice by converting some of the existing equity units into passive units and re-issuing active units to those prepared to give further concessions (as the future is now dependent upon them). It is probable that the passive units will have little value – by definition, if the company has trouble paying its debts. However, fresh units may have some value as the company should not be continuing unless a surplus is in prospect. Clearly the new contributories would not proceed with such a plan unless they were entirely happy with it, and with their ability to control it adequately to protect their interests.

It is therefore one of the strengths of the proposed model that, in adverse conditions, the corporation may well be able to continue beyond the point at which insolvency of the present limited company model would cause a cessation of trading. The reason is simply that there is an *automatic* mechanism for control to pass to those most able to contribute to the corporation's survival. If the existing share capital has been lost, then the equity units held by those persons – who controlled the company while it lost its value – are by definition of little worth, and many of them may be regarded as scrapped, so that fresh units may be issued to suppliers or employees or new investors to keep the company going while making reduced contractual payments to these new contributories. These new units will enjoy the benefit of any profits from the date of the insolvency meeting, and this gives them a meaningful value – together with, of course, the benefit of survival of the corporation upon which they all depend. Sustainability may be preserved by a relatively small reduction in costs all round. The model therefore provides for a very swift transfer of control to the most relevant contributories in such cases, and the outside market does not necessarily intrude.

In the continuing corporation, each participator automatically takes his own risk in getting paid for his own contribution: if he is unhappy, then he either must not proceed, or must insist on having adequate equity units so that he has some opportunity to exercise influence or control and have a chance to share in any profit. Those collectively controlling the equity units are in control of the enterprise; only if the enterprise has deviated from the pre-set budget or business plan can the directors be called to account. Any deviation (not just of profitability but of any pre-set commitment) from the agreed plan that might attract criticism. This gives the AGM, and the monthly meetings, real potency: it is not just a glossy account of the past, but an objective and worthwhile analysis of variations from the previously agreed budget, and a meaningful forecast of performance for the coming year in the full knowledge that failure to deliver will have to be accounted for in due course.

Conclusion

The currently topical but vexed and unresolved issue of corporate governance needs some fresh ideas in order to knit in tightly with the other aspects of the proposed new model. Historical assumptions have to be swept aside so that we can look afresh at the whole purpose of the AGM; at the whole relationship between equity holders and the corporation; at the appointment, remuneration and supervision of the directors; and at the likely reaction of the parties to adversity and potential loss. The relationship between the legislature (the equity unit holders) and the executive (the directors) needs to be far less distant, but the closer relationship must be based on a methodical and systematic exchange of information and views, not just on anecdotal, casual and selective reference to the most friendly or most vocal faces on either side.

7 Financial reporting

What is financial reporting?
We have seen that the corporation is a framework for the organisation of economic activity within the community. It will have members of the general public as its customers, or as its workforce or suppliers. When the public deal with a sole trader like Mr John Smith or the partnership of Messrs Smith & Bloggs, they know who owns and runs the business. They can meet the man or woman they are dealing with. But with a corporation, this is an *artificial* person without a human face and without the embodiment that a human person has. Its face and its substance can only be perceived by examining published documents concerning its constitution and its financial position. The corporation is, therefore, generally perceived to have an obligation to disclose publicly, for the benefit of those dealing with it, some details at least of its financial status and performance (and certain other relevant non-financial information), and it is difficult to argue that this is not a reasonable demand. Moreover, the corporation clearly has specific obligations, of a similar but much more complex type, to its equity unit holders.

The directors are in complete day-to-day control of the business, while the body of equity unit holders has the ultimate responsibility for it. These equity unit holders – possibly through a committee of governors – have the job of monitoring and supervising all that is going on: but they are very much part-time, a few hours a month at the most, and are possibly unpaid; they are also unlikely to be specifically trained to make sense out of internal accounting systems. They may well be capable decision-makers and able non-executives, but clearly they are going to need some help in assessing the financial position of the corporation, in setting or agreeing forecasts, and in monitoring how its performance compares with forecasts. This is then the object of Financial Reporting.

Because the corporation is a framework for the organisation of economic activity, it follows that, to assist in that organisation, there is a need to monitor and control economic events as they happen. The most crucial tool for doing this has to be the existence of an accounting system. There is more than one facet to accounting:

- it can be used pro-actively to assist with costing, budgeting and project evaluation (i.e., for future purposes)

- it can be used as a means of monitoring how the business is going, enabling debts to be paid and collected, calculating the bank position, and so on (current purposes)

- it is a matter of historical record, for assessing the performance of those in command of it, for profit appropriation and taxation (past purposes).

Accounting, in its widest sense, is used by a lot of different people for a lot of different purposes. Financial reporting is just one aspect of accounting.

Financial reporting is the communication of accounting information about an entity to the persons interested in it. These persons may be those vitally interested who anxiously await the financial reports to equip them with the financial knowledge necessary to make strategic decisions concerning many thousands (or even millions) of pounds, or they may be persons more casually involved whose interest is simply to have some idea of the setting in which their life's endeavours take place; they may even be casual passers-by only potentially interested in the corporation. We therefore need to ask firstly, who it is that we are reporting to, and for what purpose. Only then can we ask what exactly this audience is likely to want; then finally we can consider what we need to produce to satisfy that need.

Historically, financial reporting evolved out of a sense of duty to the shareholders; other parties such as suppliers or employees were entirely ignored. The theory was that it was the shareholders who had entrusted their funds to the directors, and these directors now needed to account to those shareholders for their stewardship. It is only relatively recently that the proposition gained ground that parties other than shareholders ought to have a proper right to some details of the financial performance and resources of a company. But it is still firmly entrenched in both statute law and custom that auditors today only have a duty to shareholders (even where these are the same persons as the directors) and none at all to other parties, however much those others may need to rely on published accounts. Some movement away from this is gradually being seen in the substance of recent court decisions, but the structure defined in the Companies Acts is signally unchanged.

On the basis that, if the interests of those intimately involved are adequately served, then the interests of those less intimately involved can be no less adequately served, let us suggest that a form of financial reporting which is acceptable to equity holders, is probably equally suitable for most other users, unless these other users have specific needs which have to be addressed separately, such as HM Revenue & Customs. We shall therefore concentrate in this chapter on the needs of financial reporting for equity holders. The needs of the directors themselves are obviously very different, and are not considered here at all: what we are considering are the needs of those to whom the corporation's internal accounting systems are not accessible and to whom therefore financial reporting is their principal source of information.

In the context of what has already been proposed for the new model of the corporation, there will need to be two separate elements to financial reporting:

1. monthly or quarterly figures for the regular meetings between the directors and the equity holders (or the governing committee of them); and

2. some form of annual report to be more carefully and thoroughly prepared than the figures in (1), and to be made available to interested parties generally.

The needs of the persons attending the meetings referred to in (1) above will be fairly specific and are likely to change in nature according to circumstances. They will in any event be relatively easy to define between the parties, being such timely information of broad reliability as will enable the users to monitor and supervise the monthly or quarterly operations of the corporation in conjunction with the board of directors. The precise details are not considered further here.

What will the users of the annual report want to see?

As was set out in chapter 6, at the previous AGM the directors will have been appointed or re-appointed with a specific mandate based largely on the business plan and forecast that was presented by them and agreed by the equity holders. At the following AGM, therefore, a financial report of some sort will need to be presented and, logically, this report should follow the pattern of the business plan so as to illustrate how well or how badly it has been accomplished. The whole picture to be examined by interested parties then consists of the details of the last AGM and presentation, the subsequent report, and the directors' proposals to be presented at the next AGM.

It was suggested in Chapter 2 that an economic enterprise is set up and run for the purpose of satisfying the economic needs of a portion of the community. The desire for each participant to 'make money' out of this, does naturally follow from it, but the principal concerns of the financial report must be, not to measure performance according to a scale of benefit to a *single* class of participant (e.g., 'what the capital provider makes out of it'), but to assess the success of the *corporation* in achieving its stated objects. These will be not just the general objects specified in its constitution (if any), but the more specific objects agreed at the last AGM. As we saw earlier in this book, these could extend beyond the traditional aims of relentless growth in turnover, profits or market share – none of which, one might suggest, are so hallowed as to be beyond question as worthy primary goals – to improving quality of service or supply, reducing staff turnover, increasing productivity, keeping prices competitive, encouraging third world economies, reducing the corporation's own environmental damage: whatever specific aims or objects had previously been set by the equity holders. Targets will have been set and, presumably, so will the criteria against which the corporation's subsequent success in achieving them might be measured.

The principal test of the financial report will then be the extent to which it enables interested parties to assess (a) the corporation's success in achieving its stated objects (i.e., the past), and (b) the corporation's general substance, resources and potential for achieving fresh objects, or achieving the same objects in a fresh way (i.e., the future). The impact of external economic or political factors, and of unexpected limitations in resources, will need to be identified by the directors as mitigating factors, which they will of course present as lucidly as possible in their favour at the AGM – to be published along with their forecast for the following year.

The financial report will need to recognise the changed format of the corporation, in that the most relevant income figure is not the 'net profit' for the shareholder, so much as the 'value added'. The report will also have to satisfy three separate needs:

- to be an objective report on how well the corporation is doing and what it is capable of – the corporation's report on itself;

- to be a historical record of performance for other purposes, such as for allocation of value added among equity unit holders, and for calculation of tax liabilities;

- to be a report on the directors themselves: how much their remuneration was, how well they installed and maintained accounting and internal control systems, and to what extent they fulfilled their statutory and contractual responsibilities generally.

The existing arrangements

Under the present system, the directors report on themselves (yes, honestly!). They prepare the entirety of their own financial report, presenting everything in the way they choose. There are two controls over this remarkable arrangement, namely (a) a complex set of rules which specify the detailed form of the financial report, with further rules which govern the content, and (b) the use of external auditors whose sole duty is to confirm that the directors have complied with all those rules.

Current financial reporting under the existing model exists somewhat symbolically as a rather passive element in the supervisory/control function by the shareholders. In reality it can be seen, in the context of public companies, as little more than a tool to aid analysts to price shares and recommend buy/hold/sell decisions. Very little if any practical control over the directors is actually exercised by the shareholders on the basis of annual published accounts. There is obviously a huge conceptual gap to be bridged here as we move away from the ability of dissatisfied equity holders to simply 'cop out' and sell their shares, towards the active control and monitoring of the corporation by its participators.

It must be said that, in recent decades, the urge for stock market analysts to make extensive comparisons in subject companies has driven the impetus of financial reporting towards an obsession about comparability and enforced standardisation of accounting policies, as if it were the primary goal of financial reporting to help the capital investor to make a short-term buy/hold/sell decision. Some would say that, in proper legal terms, that is *precisely* what the primary goal of financial reporting is at the present time. While this may be perfectly proper for this limited purpose, it is a dangerously narrow perspective. In the context of a system supposedly intended to call management to account, the concentration on 'cop out' decisions (i.e., whether to simply ditch shares and walk away when the company's performance is of any concern) says it all. If the financial report is to be a useful tool for monitoring and supervision, then it needs to be focused as much on the subject company as on comparison with competitors.

It is possible that comparability and standardisation of the presentation of financial results can sometimes get in the way of truly appropriate reporting. The need for analysts to handle large volumes of information on different companies has resulted in a tendency, not always towards a more truly comprehensive appreciation, but sometimes to the reduction of corporate performance to an absurdly tiny handful of key indicators: share price, earnings per share, dividend yield, net profit before tax, turnover, net assets. Each of these indicators can mask all sorts of underlying factors, and can be liable to distortion due to accounting and presentational judgement. It has to be said that share price – while by definition a meaningful matter when you actually buy or sell a share – is for continuing investors really little more than an opinion poll or approval rating, and can be seriously misleading. As far as the other indicators are concerned, they can become over-simplistic portrayals of performance measurement when they become (as they are bound to) targets which guide the motivation of corporate policy-makers.

It is obvious that companies which tend to 'do the right things' generally, do succeed in the market, and therefore do expand and there is a growth in turnover, value added, share price, and so on

– but this is because comprehensively successful management leads to sound economic results, not the other way round.

A detailed analysis of the specific form the financial part of the annual report might need to take in order to satisfy the new requirements of unit holders is beyond the scope of this preliminary book, but there are a handful of comments to be made.

The accounts

With regard to the income statement, this needs to provide details of the year's performance, but also in the form of a value added statement. In other words, it has to set out the sales to customers (i.e., amounts coming in from the market), less the amounts paid for bought-in goods and services (i.e., amounts paid back to the market), with the difference being the value added that is attributable to the participators in the corporation. This is the amount that (after taxation) can then be shared among the participators.

Apart from the detailed income statement showing the income and expenditure in all the traditional categories, and the overall value added, it would seem to be valuable for it to quantify (in a separate note if necessary) the level of purchases from those holding equity units as opposed to purchases from the market. The reason for this is two-fold: (a) a high level of purchases from unit holders indicates a relatively high level of flexibility in difficult times, and there is value in demonstrating this fact; and (b) unit holders are an integral part of the corporation, and the extent of their presence among cost providers may be relevant in assessing the extent of possible discount being received at the present time.

As far as the 'value added' element of the income statement is concerned, no extra accounting records should be needed. The statement is easily prepared by extracting figures in the usual way from the standard form of 'trial balance'. Anyone who can understand an income statement will be able to understand a value-added statement, particularly as it lends itself to easy presentation in graphical form too. In addition, the statement can set out the proportion of surplus being shared out among equity unit holders.

The corporation exists in the market, and its accounts must be relevant to that market. The income statement shows the purchases from the market and the sales back to the market. This will therefore show the value added by the corporation's activities over the accounting period. Similarly, the balance sheet might well need to reflect market prices: it is even possible to have two columns of figures, one the traditional historic cost price of the fixed assets and the other stated at resale prices, to provide information in connection with a potential change in direction – the 'get out value'.

The financial forecast for the following year would seem to be best left, not as part of the objective annual report, but as part of a second document which is the directors' own submission for approval at the AGM: it is part of their 'manifesto', to be considered and amended as necessary in conjunction with the equity holders, and not part of an independent report on the past.

Who should carry out this financial reporting function? The system in present use in the UK is a rather peculiar one that gives the duty to the directors, subject to an examination by the auditors. Before we can understand the problems that this creates, we need to understand how we have arrived at the present practice.

The traditional concept of auditing

The original joint stock company developed into statutory companies, and then finally into registered limited liability companies about 180 years ago, and throughout this time, investors would put their money and faith into the hands of directors for them to manage as they thought fit, leaving the directors to account for this in due course. It was not until 1908, however, that it became compulsory to publish a balance sheet; and 1929 before it was mandatory to circulate the profit and loss account among shareholders. It must then have seemed natural that the directors' account of the company's performance should be independently checked and verified in some way. It was to fulfil this function that the idea of the auditor was conceived.

Originally the 'auditor' – Latin for 'listener' – was a simple ticker and checker who listened to the calling over of double entries, and examined supporting vouchers, to verify that bookkeeping entries were correct. We can imagine that the task was almost entirely mechanical, and there was little or no need for professional judgement at that time. 'Double entry' bookkeeping ensured that profit and loss accounts and balance sheets articulated with each other, and the accounts themselves were little more than lists of nominal and private ledger balances. The auditor's role was directed to enable him to reach the simple yet formidable conclusion 'audited and found correct'.

When today someone is asked to examine a statement of income to show the profit or loss made on a fete at the local village hall, he turns to the traditional mechanical concept of auditing, and the matter is virtually black and white. There is little more to it than vouching the correctness of the entries and checking that the numbers add up. There are unlikely to be any practical alternative policies; any two accountants will almost certainly produce identical figures. This, it seems, was the basis of the approach to auditing when the concept was first introduced: it was only right and proper that the shareholders (who might never see 'the books') had someone independent whom they could trust to check all the entries to confirm that the final accounts prepared by the directors were indeed true and fair. Above all, though, it was a practical proposition that one accountant (employed by the directors) prepared the figures and another (technically employed by the shareholders) checked them.

What this illustrates, however, is that financial reporting arose as a by-product of laborious handwritten bookkeeping processes. The individual accounting entries were systematically arranged into the nominal ledger according to their nature as either 'revenue' (income statement) or 'capital' (balance sheet) items. Such mechanical work is easily audited. No specific attention was at that time given to matters of judgement in relation to unusual (even contrived) leases, financing arrangements or commercial payments to secure benefits which could extend beyond a single accounting period. Nor was much attention given to what value the final accounts were for the following purposes:

- the income statement being a valid measure of the income arising in the period and how this might guide the reader to form a valid opinion on likely future income, or

- the balance sheet being a meaningful statement of resources or net worth, which might help the reader to make an informed judgement on the company's future income performance and possible alternatives.

These much more worthwhile accounts are far more a matter of judgement – and the problem is compounded by other issues of comparability, both between enterprises (consistency in presentation) and between different time periods (consistency in currency values), which one suspects were not originally an issue to concern readers of accounts a century or more ago. More and more evidence is coming to light to suggest that the traditional approach to financial reporting (i.e., giving to the directors all the scope there is in the preparation and presentation of accounts) is failing to satisfy modern expectations, largely because these expectations have moved so far away from where they were when the concept of financial reporting was first introduced.

We all accept that in the board of directors we have a body with absolute day-to-day control over the management of an enterprise, including the setting up and operation of the whole accounting system, as well as all the internal controls to ensure that the system works; and that self-same body has the duty to prepare a statement of its own performance. In such a case of natural conflict of interest, there is an overwhelming argument that there must be some form of objective independent examination. Such an examination must, inter alia, check that the accounting system is itself adequate, that the internal controls work, and that the final published accounts agree with the underlying records. Furthermore, all the individual entries must (to a material degree at least) be true and the final statement must be 'fair' as well as true (i.e., it must be true in spirit, and overall presentation, as well as individual fact). Thus has the annual audit evolved into the extensive examination that it is today. While the audit report itself always was, and still is, very brief, at least the depth of the examination necessary gave the user of accounts some confidence that an outsider had delved deeply into the accounting records and was generally happy with them.

But all that is historical, so let us put it to one side.

What do we need today for our new concept of the corporation? We still have the directors in complete day-to-day command of the corporation, with the other participators very much on the outside. Even if the body of these participators, through the equity holders or governors, meet the directors monthly or quarterly to examine reports and budgets, do they still need some further assurances? One has to say that they do. The need for auditors of some description is still there, simply because the directors' principal concern – and what they are paid to do – is to forward manage the corporation, while it is a quite separate and conflicting function to critically appraise past performance and monitor the present. Where is the logic in the directors reporting on themselves?

The examination by auditors is quite naturally confined to accountancy (in its widest sense), while for those to whom they report, the issues on which independent reporting would be valued do extend beyond accountancy to a complete impartial review of the manner in which the company's affairs have been conducted, even perhaps to an assessment of managerial strengths and weaknesses in general. Now the auditors may indeed form worthwhile opinions on these matters in the course of their work, but it would be a very fair criticism that – in the circumstances auditors exist at present – such opinions might not be entirely valid as auditors are not necessarily adequately equipped to exercise the required judgement. This may be something to strive for, but would have to be a long term project for the profession to face in the decades to come. Yet to confine themselves to accountancy is perhaps not to demean the auditors' role as much as might at first be thought. Accountancy is, after all, the very language of business and virtually all of the strategic and operational activities of an undertaking are expressed at some stage in accounting terms, whether past, present or future, and accountants are experienced in handling and assessing the financial or economic implications of these matters.

There has been a significant development over the last few decades which has dramatically shaken the apparent value of auditing, for large companies in particular, and for which no really effective solution has yet been offered. This development is in the – often deliberately intended – sophistication of financial arrangements and accounting policies to such a degree that, for a company of any material size, it will generally now be possible for any two accountants to produce starkly different figures for profit or loss and for asset or liability, depending on whether they wish the results to look good or bad. The accountancy profession has worked very hard indeed to find ways of dealing with this by establishing all sorts of standard accounting practices, much more rigid rules which reduce the subjectivity of accounting, so that the opportunity for professional judgement is traded off against the desire for mechanical comparability and objective certainty. The rules change constantly to keep them up to date. But is this the best approach?

Perhaps the root of the problem is the auditing profession's obsession with its historically passive role, and the legislature's insistence that the direction of auditors' responsibility is to the limited aims of a single class of participant. The world of financial reporting has certainly moved on over the years and yet the basic function of the auditor has not been the subject of radical reassessment since it was first conceived: that needs to change.

A fresh look at auditing

One way in which the auditors can be seen to go wrong is that they do not actually do what most outsiders think they do: the accounts, although signed by the directors, bear the name of only one accountant – the auditor – and yet the accounts aren't actually *his*.

It is in fact the directors who are asked to report upon their own performance; to prepare and package their own accounting presentation and to exercise their own judgement for their own purposes, with the auditors simply reporting that this is *within the rules* and is 'a' *true and fair view*. Is that really what should happen? How would you feel if your solicitor took – and asked you to pay a substantial fee for – Counsel's Opinion on a matter and received in return a rigidly standard single page of opinion that merely stated that the solicitor's view was (a) within the rules and (b) one acceptable view of the matter?

The Economist recently maintained that the auditing profession had 'set the bar too low' – so that it was 'all but impossible for them to fail at their jobs' (*The Economist*, 13th December 2014). Perhaps what is at the heart of the public's complaint against auditors at the present time is *that they can only give limited assurances that the accounts aren't actually untruthful and unfair*.

Think about the possibilities that are wasted. Once a year, into every significant UK company, is sent a team of highly trained, experienced, and independent professionals, who, with all necessary authority, get to the very heart of the business and feel the whole sense and direction of the operation, and have the statutory obligation to make an independent report directly to the equity holders outside the direct management of the enterprise... and with what outcome? Well, for decades the totality of their findings was expressed (as their 'opinion') as a single written sentence, then more recently, in a single written page, virtually every word of which was strictly prescribed in advance. For accounting periods beginning on or after 1 October 2012, we now have a new long-form report, but still the contents of this are regarded (in the profession) as likely to become standardised as 'boilerplate' text.

There is a compelling case to be made for the auditor to be selected and appointed by the governors on behalf of the equity holders, and thereby of the whole body of participators, without reference to the directors, and to be charged with the simple positive duty of making his *own* objective report directly to them. He should prepare and present the accounts that bear his name. After all, if there is anyone who is a specialist at objective financial reporting, it is surely the auditor. As the properly appointed representative of all the parties having an interest in the affairs and conduct of the company, the auditor should receive the directors' management accounts and then fearlessly and independently exercise *his own best personal judgement* in preparing and presenting to the AGM not just *a* true and fair view, but *the* truest and fairest view of the financial position and trading results, so that the entire financial statements become the audit report. The auditors of most small companies already approach this ideal as a matter of routine at the present time, as they tend to prepare the final statutory accounts themselves as well as auditing them; and they are perhaps more appreciated as a result.

It seems such a pity for such expertise to be so close to the heart of the company and for such little use to be made of it. There is a public misconception that the 'clean' audit report (i.e., the expression of an opinion that the accounts are properly prepared and are true and fair) is somehow an assurance to all parties interested in a corporation that the directors in command of it are carrying out their duties honourably and effectively, that they are meeting their statutory and contractual obligations, and that their accounts are the true and fair view of everything that has happened. Privately the auditor of every company knows the truth about all these matters, inside out: if he doesn't, then he hasn't done his job properly. This, therefore, is the point: that if there is a failure on the part of good auditors, it lies not so much in their work as in their reluctance (or lack of custom and authority) to actually communicate it to the users of accounts.

A positive duty for the auditor to report objectively in his own way would seem to be the most simple and effective solution. Instead of the auditor giving a passive opinion that someone else's presentation is merely legal (i.e., complies with the regulations and is not untruthful or unfair), he will have to *justify* not only that the accounts show the truest and fairest view, but also that their presentation is the most appropriate one for all the specific circumstances of the subject company. The duty upon him will be significantly greater. Even if he falls short, he will be doing far more than at present, to the great benefit of all the users of those financial statements.

Such an annual report would have to include the adequacy of information systems and internal controls, illegal and fraudulent acts, the company's ability to meet its obligations, and many similar issues. Much progress has been made very recently towards such disclosures, but none of these give the primary duty of preparing the published accounts to the auditors.

If the auditors are to be the primary and independent financial observer, then they should logically be present in person at the corporation's AGM, so as to be able to answer honestly, independently and forthrightly, any legitimate enquiries on the report and accounts that they present. Their heightened role would have the added benefit of providing some comfort that the directors' responses at the AGM are more likely to be fair if the auditor is allowed to otherwise comment on them.

There is no denying the powerful position that directors find themselves in, and yet, if they are to do their job properly, that is unavoidable. The most effective solution must be to upgrade the auditors' function to a more positive and constructive role, so as to be in more sympathetic balance with the more positive role of the equity holders. This should bring more authority, democracy and effectiveness to the overall control of the corporation by

- vesting that control in the most relevant participators,

- focusing it in the hands of an effective governing committee, and

- having the constructive audit function intrinsic to the work of the governing committee.

Some arrangement under which the auditors were actually selected and paid by the governors, instead of by the directors, perhaps with the anticipated audit fee being set aside for them over the course of the year, would also contribute to this.

Are there any cost implications in this change of attitude for the auditor? The auditors already carry out an extensive examination of all the accounting records, in effect checking – even if only by sampling the system where appropriate – every material entry right up to the final published accounts, as part of the process of audit. It is difficult to see why, if the accounting records are adequate, which is a mandatory requirement anyway, any material increase in cost at all should result from the need for the auditor to decide upon and implement a particular accounting policy as opposed to considering the implications of a policy chosen by the directors and checking its implementation. Certainly in smaller companies, the auditor is often happier to be left to prepare the published accounts (assuming that sound management accounts are available) than to have to check and assess the presentation by somebody else. With regard to the expression of an opinion on other matters, all the underlying work for this is already carried out by the auditor of every company and painstakingly recorded by him. All that he is now being asked to do, is to publish his findings. Attending the AGM will, of course, have a small additional cost, although, to be fair, auditors have for very many years had the authority to attend the AGM even though this opportunity is not always taken up, and little practical use is made of it.

The size of any additional cost is unlikely to be material in the context of the existing fee; in contrast to the likely benefits from objectivity, from the closure of the public's expectation gap, it is minuscule. From the perspective of the user of the financial report, there would be far greater gains and the generation of rather more interest in the auditors' report. There would be market pressure on auditors to carry out this function in the best interest of the equity holders, with competition for the clearest, sharpest and most effective reports – competition in visible quality of work and output, not just on price and on friendship with the financial director.

Finally, it could be suggested that the more positive role for the auditor might lead to hostility between that person and the directors. There is certainly no evidence to suggest that there is any general hostility between directors and auditors in their present role. Perhaps that reflects a failure of objectivity in the relationship... or more likely is evidence of the diplomacy and professionalism of the auditor. But what may be perceived by directors as a mere clarification of the auditor's role – which at present is supposed to be independent anyway – is unlikely to produce actual hostility. The present practice of directors exerting pressure on auditors to encourage favourable professional judgement is unlikely to change, but it is likely to be much less effective than it is now, on the simple basis that the auditors are selected, appointed and paid by the governors, and report directly to them; and the final situation will undoubtedly be little different from the relationship which subsists between those same accountants and the tax inspector: each has a job to do and a natural desire to do it properly and professionally, and – perhaps surprisingly to some people – real hostility or irreconcilable conflict is a genuine rarity in that relationship.

8 The contribution of labour

The master/servant relationship
When considered objectively, the present concept of employment does appear to be a peculiar remnant of the feudal system. It is an anachronism in the modern market economy, for one person to be 'in service' to another, with no structure for reward other than an uncomfortable balance between confrontational pseudo-market forces and the tensions of loyalty and goodwill. It remains essentially a master/servant relationship, with emancipation only being manifest in the level of collective bargaining and in a high degree of legislative intervention. It must be said that much of this regulation irritably distorts market forces through clumsy intervention and sometimes appears to engender suspicion, alienation and confrontation as a result. In larger businesses, it discourages harmony and cohesion between management and workforce: they are made to feel as if they are on different sides. In smaller businesses, it actively discourages employment.

The proposed model has the capacity to provide for the contribution of labour in two ways, each quite different from the present system of employment. Firstly, it is expected that all members of the *core* workforce will be *structurally* involved. They will participate 'for richer or poorer' as an intrinsic part of the corporation and its governing systems. They will share in the control of the corporation and in the financial rewards for doing so – they will be *on precisely the same side* as the directors. The second type of labour contribution applies to those whose involvement is marginal to the business. Under existing arrangements, these will be the casual staff who are taken on for only a few weeks at a time, or for only a few hours in each week. Their pay needs to be adequate for them to be prepared to do this, and what they receive in such pay will obviously be all they can expect from that source: it would be impractical to treat such temporary staff as equity holders. In our proposed new model, these workers will be independent individuals having the disadvantage (along with the freedoms and benefits) of full exposure to the market place.

At present, there is a need to give permanent employees legislative protection so that the very *permanence* of their situation is recognised. That is obviously a good thing, in theory. But, while this benefits such permanent staff, its application to *all* employees is counter-productive, so that marginal or casual workers have to be made even more marginal (by means of zero-hours contracts for example) in order to evade the legislative burden. Under the new proposals, however, permanent staff will be part of the company, so the legislative burden can be made lighter on the remainder of the 'employees', and instead be made more relevant to their precise needs. Ironically, this should encourage greater use of marginal workers.

The opportunity for all sizes of business to engage staff outside the permanent strictures of rigid employment is likely to encourage the growth of employment at the margins, and at the same time reduce the pressure to replace such employees by mechanical processes. Obviously such marginal employment needs to be organised fairly, with an equality of bargaining power, and the legislation needs to focus on this.

It is a paradox that efforts made to protect employees' pension rights and to enhance employment security sometimes have the very clear result that not only is recruitment discouraged, but also more businesses may sometimes have to be closed and the jobs lost on the basis that a break-up (in order to end employment and pension rights) is more economically worthwhile for a purchaser than a going-concern sale. The solution proposed by the new model resolves this.

It is rarely appreciated just how important employees are. A company's workforce is not just the means of implementing strategic policy decisions by the directors, it is the crucial interface between the company and all those who deal with it. Outsiders, whether they are customers or suppliers, rarely have much contact with the directors, but deal constantly with employed staff. Moreover, contact between the public and a corporation is often at the *lowest* level of employment, and so the importance of the attitude and enthusiasm of such staff cannot be overstated.

The continuing success of a company depends on the quality of its workforce as much as on its directors, and that is why they both need to be on the same side, and to be structurally incorporated within the company. Granting equity units to the workforce can help to achieve this, as the new model enables the labour contribution to be recognised as an equity involvement as it stands, without staff having to pretend that they are also shareholders (as they do at present). One of the major advantages of the new system is also that the 'bonus' allocation to staff (i.e., the cash surplus they eventually share through possession of equity units) is not a *cost* for the company, but is part of the *appropriation of profit*, so it no longer appears as a cost to be minimised but is celebrated as part of a successful achievement.

The chairman of one of Britain's most successful employee-owned businesses, the John Lewis Partnership, expressed it clearly:

"There is increasing evidence that companies owned by their employees deliver higher productivity and greater levels of innovation. They are more resilient to economic downturns and have more engaged and happy workers, who are less stressed." (Mayfield 2014:33)

The market place

It is for market forces to determine who will hold equity units. In all likelihood, this will eventually extend to encompass the majority, if not all, of the permanent staff. Sadly, those employees who are marginal to the enterprise can hardly bargain for equity. The truth is as simple, cruel (in the short term) and inevitable as Darwin's principle of natural selection. So long as it is of practical advantage to the corporation to employ certain staff, those staff will be employed. Once technology, or any other business development, reduces the viability of their employment below the threshold, their job is at an end, and no amount of State intervention will alter that fact.

There are new industries and new jobs. It may no longer be necessary for human beings to be involved in the unenviable business of heavy manual exertion, the tedious business of clerical labour and the unrewarding operation of basic machinery in making things, but more and more people are being needed in those industries where being human is a distinct advantage, such as education, health care, social services, community policing, leisure, sport, recreation, entertainment, art and literature.

As already explained, the heavy legislative burden designed to improve the employees' lot is seen by many small businesses as a serious disincentive to take on marginally productive staff, and for very small employers to take on staff at all. Often it is the complexity of the employment rules and the inflexible, authoritarian demands of PAYE income tax and national insurance administration that frighten small businesses more than the reality. It has also been seen that the rules simply do not fortify the longevity of a particular job position, and are to some extent counter-productive.

If non-equity staff could be more freely available without the baggage that presently accompanies them, then it is possible that employers would be far more ready to provide a few weeks of marginal employment to many more staff – and would be less obsessed to find ways to reduce employment. Marginal employees could be offered individual work contracts, tailored to fit local needs and individual circumstances. Such employees would be encouraged to be members of trade unions, which in turn would have real traditional relevance in equalising bargaining power in agreeing the standard terms of contracts and in conducting negotiations.

A free market approach to some employees would not necessarily affect the position of those structurally engaged within the corporation; what it would do is to bring the absolute reality of market economics into employment and thereby remove some of the existing disincentives. Marginal employment is not ideal for everyone, and would need the welfare system to accommodate it, but it is better than total unemployment, and for some people (such as mothers with small children, or people doing part-time studies, or pursuing a hobby that could eventually turn into a business) it is a practical solution.

There is much discontent with the terms and conditions of marginal employment at the present time – such as a requirement for zero-hours contracts combined with a demand for exclusivity of employment. But the problem here is not exposure to market forces, rather it is in the unequal bargaining power of the two parties. With greater demand for more marginal staff, those workers would have more power to choose, and consequently to demand a fairer and more equal contract. How does that work? At present, employment is in short supply while potential workers are plentiful, so employers can demand what they want; if there were more demand for labour, there would be more competition among employers, so the terms they offer would be improved. Workers would flock to those offering the best terms, and meaner employers would be forced to improve their terms.

Promoting the labour contribution

The proposed new model of the corporation is designed to improve the position of the person contributing their labour in the following ways:

1. by bringing core employees within the corporate structure, which should slightly reduce their immediate cost (increasing their marginal use), improve their sense of participation in a meaningful way (by giving them an element of control), and eventually reward them financially as a result

2. by reducing regulatory disincentives to marginal employment, which should promote more marginal use of labour, and

3. by reducing or eliminating wages taxes, which should dramatically bring down the direct cost of labour, and thereby encourage employment.

The ideal in a modern civilised human society is that all those who seek to be economically active should have every opportunity to do so. That is why it is promoted so vigorously in our proposed new corporate structure. It is also promoted by encouraging marginal employment. But there is a third aspect, as indicated above.

We need to ask why we tax employment in the same way that we tax tobacco and alcoholic drink. We tax *those* items to discourage them... So why do we heap costs on to employment, so that the cost to the employer of a day's labour is far greater than the benefit received by the employee – thus discouraging employment? This question is addressed in chapter 12.

9 Thinking it through: some practical effects

The Stock Market

Continuing to have a *market* for capital-related equity units (in public companies) is absolutely essential. This is where people can go to invest their money, and where they can go to turn it back into cash. The existence of a public market for investment was one of the principal reasons for the success of capitalism. Far more capital will be available if capital shares can be freely traded: few individuals (and not all that many institutions) will want to invest a substantial amount in a particular public corporation for a fixed period of ten or twenty years. The opportunity to invest quite small sums for quite short periods attracts much more demand. An established market will enable such investors to invest sums of their choice for periods of their choice, and at a risk and return of their choice.

A new division of the Stock Market will therefore be required to deal with the market in *capital-only* equity units. These are the only type of equity units that would be freely tradable, as the participation that they represent is simply to provide risk capital for a pre-determined period of years, and in a public company the identity of such an investor is not necessarily relevant. Does it matter that such capital-related equity units also provide an element of control over the directors? Most short-term investors would find that irrelevant as they can 'cop out' by selling their shares (as they do at present); but longer-term investors may well be more interested. Either way, it does not particularly matter, as there will be other (non-capital) equity unit holders who are more concerned: fortunately, in our new model, control does not depend on capital investors alone.

Novel forms of pricing will have to develop for capital-only equity units in public companies. The price will need to reflect the underlying 'nominal value' of the unit (i.e., how much was originally invested in the company, and will be eventually repaid by it) and the interim rate of interest paid on that sum, plus a market view of the current potential value of the anticipated surpluses arising in which the units will share. There will be many similarities with today's market, but it may be slightly more complicated.

The principal distinguishing feature will be that the price of such equity units will not always be expected to rise, and it will no longer always be a poor reflection on the company when the price falls. The price is likely to increase shortly after issue, and then continue to rise while the corporation (or the new project for which the units were issued) becomes established. As the corporation makes surpluses, the unit prices will reflect this. But as the corporation (or its new project) reaches maturity, the price will stabilise and then slowly fall as the risk premium reduces. Among other changes, companies will be less likely to be homogenous – they will have stronger individual characteristics, as will their capital-related equity units. Brokers, or stockbrokers as they used to be called, will have to do a little more work for their money. Investors, however, will not lose out, as they will still have a varied range of investments to choose from, many of which will offer substantial returns.

What will the impact be on capital investors and how will that in turn affect the availability of investment funds? Is there a risk that, because the proposed corporate model is likely to reduce the proportion of equity available to capital providers, there will be less incentive for capital providers to put their capital at risk?

Investors should see very handsome income returns on their capital throughout the period of investment, but this period will be much more finite than it is at present, so they will need to be active investors to get the best results. The total income (interim rate of interest plus equity share) should, however, be many times greater than the current rate of dividend yield. Capital gains, on the other hand, will no longer feature so dramatically as at present, and if equity shares are acquired in their prime and then held to maturity, they may well show a capital loss.

Massive speculative gains (which add nothing to the market in terms of value-added) will become fewer and probably only apply to initial public offerings (IPOs) of capital-related equity units, where these are resold shortly after issue.

In those corporations for which capital is the principal (or even the sole) critical contributor, virtually all the equity will have to be available to pay for it. But what if the venture is not likely to show any real profit for ten years or more? There is nothing in the model to stop the equity being issued solely to risk capital providers for a fixed period of even fifty years. This would give plenty of time for the project to reach maturity, yield a good return and even have a reasonable period of 'run off' before equity gradually passes to the other participators who subsequently become of more importance to the venture.

In theory, equity in the new model could remain in the hands of capital providers for generations (as it does at present), but the point is that this would be happening because of necessary market pressures rather than by default. This might be applicable in the case of hugely capital-intensive projects such as the channel tunnel, but even here there would always be the possibility of a handful of equity units being available for other non-capital participators with a critical input – such as directors or senior marketing employees. This flexibility is vital, because even (especially?) something like a major infrastructure project needs more than just a pile of cash; it needs very sound, competent vision, planning, marketing, management and control.

As was explained in Chapter 4, there is nothing to stop risk capital providers from bargaining for the highest possible returns, and achieving them. But there would be real open market pressure to distinguish between *risk* capital and *loan* capital; and to recognise that the risk profile of venture capital does change with time, so rather more monitoring and activity would become associated with investment. They would have to do more for their money! The present volume of capital *available* for investment would be precisely the same, that won't change. But where it finds a home will depend rather more on the risk preference of the investor, and the return available on it will depend entirely on what the market is prepared to offer.

Very small enterprises
For at least half a century there have been in the UK what some have termed 'one man and a dog' limited companies – very small

businesses with only one or two directors and no outsiders – and since the Companies (Single Member Private Limited Companies) Regulations 1992 came into effect on 15 July 1992, it is now possible to form a company with just a single member. These very small companies are uniquely British – they are rare on the continent of Europe – and could be said to be an anachronism. In so far as the motivation may be to hide behind the limited liability protection, or to take advantage of lower corporate tax rates, it is difficult to see why they should be encouraged, from the point of view of the community as a whole, but sometimes there is a more responsible motivation. Perhaps the person or persons concerned have high expectations and want a form of organisation that will outlast their own lifetime, or they want something more than self-employment or partnership, because, for example, a corporate identity may be important, and yet they may not want the involvement of others in their decision-making and profit-sharing.

While the proposed model has the flexibility to accommodate such a proposition, it is arguable whether this is really appropriate. The whole basis of the proposed model is that it exists to serve a portion of the community: there is therefore much to be said for building in a structured requirement for a minimum number of equity unit holders, even if just one director is sufficient, and that as soon as there are any permanent employees, they *must* be represented among the unit holders. A very small corporation of one or two people probably exists, not so much to serve the community, but more to provide an income for those two persons, and thus is philosophically inappropriate to the proposed model.

A possible middle course might therefore be for the continuation of the existing model of the 'unlimited company', a format largely similar to the existing private limited company, but with the shareholders being fully liable for the company's debts on an insolvent winding-up. On this basis, the outsiders contract with the business on the same basis that they would do with a private individual or partnership, with no published accounts available, and yet the corporate existence still provides the conveniences of incorporation – such as perpetual existence, separation of ownership and management, the ability to own property and to sue in a company name – without at the same time affording any shelter from legitimate claims. Necessary changes to the existing rules would be minimal.

The founder of a new small enterprise needs to be an exceptional person: he or she has usually to give up considerable time and effort to start the business, with very little economic reward in the early years, and a failure rate that is truly daunting. Those who succeed on their own deserve considerable reward for it and, in an unlimited company, will continue to do so. If, however, they involve others to a significant degree, then they must begin to not just share their rewards, but involve others in decision-making – and the new model of the corporation then begins to appear more relevant as the vehicle to enable this to take place.

It could be said, perhaps somewhat romantically, that it is the present nature of proprietorial ownership of corporate activity which so attracts the truly original entrepreneur, who sometimes regards his corporate business enterprise, complete with all its employed staff, not so much as a mechanical cash production machine, but more as a creative product with a life of its own – a *dynamic* work of art of which he is the master. For such a person, the drive to maximise growth is a phenomenon similar to personal sporting achievement; actually making money is almost a by-product. While such archetypal entrepreneurs tend, by their very nature, to be rather autocratic and ill-suited to the gradual filtering down of equity control to others, nevertheless they are usually very effective businessmen; their business ventures can become very successful, and the controls structurally imposed by the new model can be far more effective than in the existing model. This is argued on the grounds that the directors would be positively and structurally supervised or controlled by the unit holders/governors, whereas under the present system there is a complete and bland delegation – often amounting to abandonment – of control to the board of directors. Furthermore, the existing feature of the absolute permanence of proprietorial ownership adds an oppressiveness to the dominance of such directors, from which the only escape is further economic wealth from another source.

It is to be hoped that the proprietors or directors of some of these very small enterprises will become represented among equity unit holders in larger enterprises, so as to contribute to the organisation of other corporations. It must be said that the current obsession about bestowing all the burdens of expert consultants and word-processed jargon – which help to nicely pad out larger companies – upon the smallest of businesses often has little more effect than to cause temporary hesitation in the pure enterprise of natural instinct. It may be more constructive to invite larger companies to shed a few professional managers and expose themselves to the raw realities of a few successful market traders. Small businesses simply do not need the burden of rigid plans and structures, which one suspects were generally designed in the first place to give small-company-like cohesion and manageability to larger enterprises, for whom the absence of small company features was a weakness! If anything, in small companies, opportunity and enterprise rather than systematic planning is the scarcest resource – and that means versatility, or as few structures as possible.

The problem of ownership: takeovers and brand value

One of the key features of the proposed new model of the corporation is that it is a framework rather than a chattel. In other words, it exists to facilitate economic activity between different parties rather than actually being the property of a specific contributor. The 'equity' *belongs* to those making the present strategic contributions to the corporation, but they don't *own* it in the sense of being able to sell it. This is a critical distinction. If a corporation can't be owned, then it can't be the wholly-owned subsidiary of another corporation either. There are several implications that follow from this. The implications of growth by acquisition are dealt with in the next section, but for the present let us focus on the implications for the company itself.

If a company cannot be bought and sold, then the proposed system of equity units would help a corporation to preserve its integrity by preventing, to a large degree, the practice of predatory take-overs. Under the present system, publicly-quoted companies are vulnerable to such hostile take-overs on the basis that share ownership gives title to all that a business is and does. There is nothing in the proposed model to restrict beneficial organic growth, i.e., the expansion of a corporation by simply getting bigger. But the practice of growth by acquisition, or by the exchanging of shares in the victim company for shares in the predatory company, can have the effect of concentrating large amounts of resources very quickly into fewer hands, while eliminating healthy competition at the same time.

One day this sort of activity may become regarded as being as distasteful as the expansion of an empire by acquiring more overseas colonies. Certainly it could be compared to a reduction of biodiversity in nature; its purpose is purely short-term advantage and efficiency, but only from the point of view of the capital provider (together with some prestige for the directors of the larger company), without any consideration necessarily being given to the wider interests of all those affected. It is now widely accepted that concentration on monoculture in nature – while at first seemingly very efficient – is not actually in the best long-term interests of any of us, and one can only wonder whether the same conclusion may eventually be reached about the concentration of manufacturing or trading into fewer and fewer large monoliths, for whom service to and awareness of the general community becomes progressively and necessarily more remote.

Another problem which is also a direct result of the existing proprietorial concept of share capital, is the way in which the sale of an existing company's shares represents a process one might call 'skin swapping': a successful venture becomes established and grows, thanks to good staff, good suppliers and good management – and a good niche in the market, or a good product – and develops a 'skin' which is the external perception of the business, as reinforced by trade names, brands and logos. In the traditional model, the shareholders can be tempted by the prospect of a quick capital gain, and the shares pass to an absolute beginner or even a competitor in the same trade, who then puts on the vendor's skin. The competitor, however, is freely able to change suppliers for cheaper ones, to reduce product quality, and to replace directors and senior management, while hoping that the community will not notice, because he uses the old company's name, logo and brands.

This feature of present companies could fairly be said to be the denial of the integrity of a business: the substance of the business should support the corporate image and the brand name – as the public is led to believe through advertising – and it seems improper to disconnect it from the product and quietly put it in the shareholders' pockets as soon as it develops value. Unless the product or service represented by the corporation or the brand is truly transferable, it does no credit to the whole concept of corporate image and brand names. It shows contempt for the general consumer public, and it provides the directors with an incentive to excessively satisfy the needs and wishes of the current shareholders, instead of having proper regard for the long-term interests of the corporation itself.

The proposition that the shell of a successful company can be routinely sold and quietly filled by competitors is as ugly as the proposition that a successful brand name is a valuable commodity separable from the organisational inputs that actually created and represent it. Some cynic might suggest that university degrees, knighthoods or any other personal honour, reputation or achievement is a saleable commodity to be traded for cash as soon as it has been legitimately bestowed. Who would regard Poland under Soviet domination as the very same country as the present Poland? It is as absurd to imagine that a nation state could be saleable (or buyable), as much as members of one's family. Even when a new 'tribute' band takes on the music and behaviour of another, however similar it is, it is still regarded as a very poor substitute for the real thing.

Brands and reputations exist to reflect what's behind them, what created them, not the other way round. Something like a reputation may *belong* to you, without you actually *owning* it, as if it were some saleable chattel, and this misunderstanding is at the heart of the malaise affecting corporate economic activity. It is deeply insidious too: recently the English National Health Service (NHS) accident and emergency service – known as the 'A&E' – was described by an insider as a 'successful brand', as if all the problems of the NHS might be solved if only all doctors' surgeries (and perhaps the local High Street pharmacy) were re-named A&E. It is the underlying hospital system that is successful, whatever name it goes under, not the brand or label that is the shorthand description for it, and the brand will be worthless unless what it represents is as good as the original.

Growth and expansion

The equity unit holders hold their equity units because their particular contribution has required that they play a part in overseeing the control of the corporate entity, and because they will only give their contribution at the agreed price provided that they share in any surplus which results.

Control, however, is not quite the same as *ownership*, as has been explained above. A corporation is an artificial being, and so it needs human management to control it; but at the same time, it is a legal 'person' in its own right – possessing bundles of rights and responsibilities – and it is therefore not entirely appropriate that any other person should actually own it; after all, a child may belong to its parent (who controls it), but the parent does not *own* the child. The equity holders may own the residual surpluses, but not (strictly) the corporation itself. This point is important as the purpose of the corporation is to serve a portion of the community, and in particular its participators, as a framework for economic activity; for it to do this with integrity, it should strictly be independent of all its participators, and in particular not be owned by any one of them. The implications of this are profound: apart from anything else it would preclude the present practice of having pyramids of holding companies and subsidiaries. There is nothing to prevent any one company from partaking in the establishment of many others and enjoying equity participation as a result, but that is quite different from having wholly-owned subsidiaries.

How would the proposed new model of the corporation deal with those situations when, at present, a corporation decides that it needs to create a subsidiary company?

Sometimes, a new enterprise is ring-fenced within a subsidiary in order to protect the main company from the claims of creditors in the event of insolvency. As argued in the next chapter, this could to some extent be seen as an abuse of the system: if those owning and in charge of the operation are not prepared to face the consequences of failure, then why should outside suppliers?

On other occasions, a subsidiary is formed so that the results of a particular section of business can be isolated and the managers rewarded for the specific results of that section. There is nothing to stop different sections of a business having separate accounting systems so that their results can be isolated; neither is there anything to stop bonuses being paid to specific managers or sales staff calculated on their particular performance. You don't need a separate company to do that. Part of the bonus can be by way of equity units in the overall entity: an excellent idea is to remind *all* staff that it is the performance of the corporation as a whole that matters, rather than just their individual section of it.

How would a corporation with equity units deal with expansion? It would have other opportunities. As an example, let us examine the ways in which a new model corporation (assuming it was already established) might expand, such as in the establishment of a new hotel complex:

1. *organic expansion*: the existing corporation buys the new site, borrowing cash as necessary (on secured or unsecured loans, or even by issue of risk capital plus equity units) to carry out the development. It then runs the hotel as part of its existing business, producing (if desired) separate accounts for that particular venture as it represents an identifiably separate activity. By having the venture as part of the corporation, there is integrity in the promotion of the corporation's name – in direct contrast to the present position with a wholly-owned subsidiary whose holding company (while offering apparent substance and authority to the subsidiary) may actually take no legal responsibility whatever for its subsidiary's debts and obligations; or

2. *promotion*: the existing corporation may provide the initial start-up funds as risk capital (plus of course a substantial share of equity units during the start-up period) in a fresh corporation set up specifically for the new hotel. This new corporation is then an autonomous corporation in its own right, but a major portion of its profits will initially go, quite reasonably, to the risk capital provider; or

3. *contractual support*: the existing corporation can provide not just capital, but management assistance, or perhaps offer a contractual franchise arrangement so that the new hotel has a common style with the existing corporation. Again the new venture will be a corporation in its own right, and its directors must always act in the best interests of itself, without regard to the external corporation. In addition, there will be equity units held by persons (particularly employees once the venture becomes well-established) other than the capital providers. The influence of the 'parent' corporation will depend on the extent and *continuance* of its contribution to the new entity. It could have substantial equity units in the new enterprise (as well as charging a rental fee), but the critical point is that these equity units would not last forever: they would need to be actively renewed every so often, and for that to happen, the contribution attaching to them would need to continue.

There is, however, nothing in the proposed new model that prevents two or more corporations simply combining together into one larger operation by merging their net assets and their equity units. Clearly, this would require a substantial consensus among the equity unit holders, including both staff and capital providers, for example, as their liability and rewards would be changing significantly. It would also have to be a *complete* merger with existing equity holders swapping their current units for fresh equity units in the new larger enterprise, and the separate identities of the two companies would be merged. It is in this way that an 'unequal' merger could still take place, and this is the reason why it was stated at the start of the previous section that hostile takeovers would only be prevented 'to a large degree'. Individual companies would not be bought and sold, but their net assets could be merged (or those of the smaller one could be subsumed into a larger company) and the equity units swapped for fresh units in the larger combined enterprise. How does this differ from a takeover? Very significantly: it is not just remote and uninvolved shareholders who decide to make more money by selling their shares to another company, it is the most involved parties in the corporation – including the staff – who decide together to merge their business with another. A decision by all those most critically involved in a corporation is quite different from a decision made remotely over the heads and behind the backs of those same participants.

Minority interests
One of the significant failings of the existing private limited company is the feeble position of the minority shareholder. This person may have invested substantial capital in the company, and yet can be dismissed as a director (if such he or she was) and will then have little or no voice whatever. The remaining directors – representing all the other shareholders – can then vote themselves substantial salaries and bonuses, leaving no profit available for distribution as a dividend to the shareholders. Such minority shares can therefore become virtually worthless, and the position can become a source of misery for the minority shareholder involved, who to all intents and purposes has been frozen out.

There are remedies under the UK Companies Acts, making provision for either a compulsory winding-up or some alternative 'just and equitable' remedy, but either the suffering shareholder needs to have originally been an active participator (a 'quasi-partner') with the other shareholders, or else needs to be suffering what has to be shown to have been clear *oppression* as a minority shareholder at the hands of the majority – and in both cases, he or she needs to have the resources necessary to bring and sustain a legal action in the High Court. The best and most common solution in practice is not a remedy but a prevention – the drawing up of a proper shareholders' agreement even before the company first starts to trade.

How does the proposed model deal with this particular problem? For a start, the fragmentation of share ownership – such as happens in family companies, when shares are inherited by distant cousins and in-laws, and family differences and rivalries lead to feuds, with the random assembly of a team not selected for their contributions – should not happen. By that time, the corporation should have repaid its initial share capital, or at least the equity units necessary for it should be insignificant, and the equity will only be in the hands of active participators, as selected by the directors. In that sense, they will *all* be 'quasi-partners'. Secondly, the equity unit holders will change periodically according to the needs of the business, so that blocks of active equity units should not normally get inherited or be the subject of matrimonial disputes. Thirdly, perhaps most importantly, each issue of equity units is in itself part of a contractual arrangement, and the prospective unit holder has the opportunity to specify his own terms for that contract. There is therefore no reason why *all* equity units cannot be issued with a standard short form of 'unit holders agreement' covering the most relevant aspects likely to be in dispute – including, for example, the maximum remuneration payable to the board of directors, and to what extent the units are transferable. This is possible with active equity units because they are issued individually and then cancelled when the contribution ceases. Shares, on the other hand, may pass endlessly by transfer or transmission and therefore, unless there is a pre-existing shareholders' agreement which caters for the transmission and fragmentation of the holdings, a subsequent shareholder has no power to call for a suitable agreement, and the directors are disinclined to provide one to a person whose active involvement they no longer seek.

The threshold of economic viability
With larger corporations, we sometimes see what seems to be inexplicable, such as the closure of a modestly successful part of the operation. This failing portion (such as a particular retail store – let us call it a project) may actually be 'viable' in the sense that it has the capacity to survive, i.e., to sustain itself and those operating it. However, the corporation applies a quite different test to decide whether or not to continue it. The test is not just whether there is likely to be a *surplus* after all costs have been met, so that the project adds to the company's profits, but something tougher: the *quality* of the earnings arising. Because the project will inevitably involve some capital, the surplus needs to be expressed as *a return* on that capital. If this rate of return is positive, but low, then to continue the project would dilute the existing rate of return on the corporation's total capital employed. Accordingly, the project fails the test, and would normally be rejected on the grounds that the quality of earnings is insufficient: it would cause the company's share price to fall, because each £1 of share capital would produce a lower percentage return than if the project were excluded.

When evaluating a project, a business needs to maximise what it gets out of those resources that are the most limited. Perhaps it's shelf space, floor area, staff available, or frontage on the High Street; with the capitalist mindset, it's always the amount of capital employed. If capital is the one and only critical contributor to business, then tests designed to encourage only the most competitively successful projects for that capital, will bring about the best overall results for economic activity. But capital is *not* the only strategic factor in business, indeed it would be perfectly accurate to suggest that for large successful businesses in the western world, capital is not the most limited resource at all: that suggestion is almost a creative fiction when huge sums languish on deposit earning 1% or 2% interest, even in the balance sheets of those self-same companies! If for a moment we were to question whether it was considered critical that as many people as possible should be involved in economic activity, then it is obvious that an entirely different test would be appropriate.

Let us assume that those people operating the project (whether investing capital, labour or other contribution) are prepared to accept (as a minimum) just a living wage or other basic return for their contribution. Then, if the project is capable of producing a surplus after paying all the other market costs in full, plus the basic return to the participators, there *will* be a positive surplus. The *quality* of earnings is not relevant, so long as it is positive, and so long as the capital (and other factors) needed for the project can be serviced. Value will have been added to goods or services bought in from the market, and a surplus will result when they are returned to the market. In the view of those people who are otherwise without gainful occupation, that project would be viable because it gives them a sufficient living wage (or other return) plus the prospect of an eventual bit of surplus as well. This, after all, is how the smallest self-employed people survive. Few of them are fortunate enough (initially at any rate) to be able to question the 'quality' of their earnings, provided they are adequate for their purposes – with that adequacy often being based on need rather than preference.

Under this book's proposals for corporate organisation, the simple 'value added' test of viability would be natural and automatic, and as a result it is likely that very many more marginal projects would be found acceptable. This in turn is likely to result in the creation of more employment and, overall, an increase in economic growth. Lots of small positive sums add up to a number much greater than zero.

What would be the effect on competitors in the market place and on the general economy? There would be no reduction in the pressure to keep costs down (because a surplus still needs to be made, and participators are always wishing to improve themselves), and it would drive up total output (as there would be more value added for the same working population), thus improving economic growth and the benefit to the consumer. The total amount of economic activity would increase, as many of those people otherwise unemployed would be doing jobs that were producing a surplus above the cost of their labour, i.e., adding value to the economy generally. Government expenditure would go down as unemployment (and thus welfare costs) would fall. Furthermore, many of the jobs could well involve repair or reclamation which, while labour intensive, is often valuable in reducing the demand for scarce raw materials. In that sense, by attributing a greater economic price to natural assets (discussed later in this book) and a lower price on human labour, there would be greater consumption of human labour, i.e., less unemployment. In providing more effective competition to improve the productive efficiency of technology, labour would be fighting back instead of just giving up. And all because of a different economic framework.

The inability to see business projects from a balanced viewpoint rather than from the distorted perspective of just the capital provider is a crucially important failure of the existing model, and the implications of this fault extend far beyond the mere viability of projects. It is part of the whole problem of the inability to recognise the input of a wider range of stakeholders in economic activity. The significance of this has also been made clear by Prof David Hatherly in his 'Stakeholder Capital Maintenance Theory' (Hatherly: 2014). Under his proposals, the phenomenon is dealt with by accounting corrections through a stakeholder fund, something that can be effectively applied to any corporation, including existing ones. The proposals in this book, however, seek to solve the problem at source by means of a corporate framework that prevents the issue arising in the first place, so that the effects do not need subsequent correction.

It is ironic that, in the context of economic activity existing for the overall good of mankind, by means of a global market for division of labour, the traditional corporate structure ostensibly treats human employment as a source of irritation, and a negative cost to be minimised or even eliminated – such that corporate management is constantly motivated to avoid extending employment if at all possible. The traditional model of economic viability is entirely inappropriate to the needs of the present day. It is like having a vehicle with a single speed gearbox – full speed ahead or dead stop – when it should ideally be infinitely variable with as smooth a progression as possible, to cope with short-term obstacles and to mollify the effects of longer term decline, where that is inevitable in a particular industry.

Do equity holders know what's good for them?
The proposed corporate model would shift the nominal control of a corporation from the shareholders (who have a well-defined and established financial motivation) to a general body of equity holders whose motivation is likely to be more broadly based. It could be argued that this empowerment of those not previously enfranchised may lead to some weak or misguided leadership. Is this likely to be a problem?

The specific risk is that while people do tend to know what's good for them, the market mechanism, being intensely individualistic, does not always deliver this. For example, villagers may express the earnest wish to retain the existence of their local general store and would truly regret its loss, yet they still individually drive to the town supermarket because it is cheaper, fresher and has more choice. The local shop is only patronised in emergencies, and accordingly cannot survive. Similarly the voting population may know full well that higher taxes are required to fund a decent education, health service and so on, but they instinctively vote against it when put to the test in a voting booth. The population wants civilised values, quality of culture and environment and so on, but individually, people will only choose this if they know that everyone else does too – and even then, they assume everyone else will do the right thing, so that they don't have to.

This 'free rider' syndrome is therefore the risk. The autocratic boss overcomes this by imposing what he regards as the right decisions, and then tolerates a contented grumble: the individuals resolve their conflict by transferring their conscience to the leader and venting their feelings against him – moaning interminably about the authorities is psychologically more comfortable (and easier) than being good on one's own conscience.

The answer in the context of the proposed model is that the equity holders will not normally exercise control individually and anonymously from a remote source, such as a polling booth. They will in general be exercising control as a board of governors. And it is a fair observation that a committee overcomes the problem by encouraging the public airing of the more virtuous thoughts and by inducing, or shaming, individual members to suppress their more selfish motives. It is easier to agree on matters beneficial to a group when the decision is being made collectively by the group.

It is also probably right to say that democracy *does* work in politics. It is overly patronising to suggest that individuals cannot make what they think is the right decision. One benefit with democracy is that people get what they deserve, and in the long run that has to be the only way forward.

It is possible that not all boards of governors will focus on economic growth as the principal priority of their corporate endeavours. The proposed model permits corporations to be, let us say, more human, and human aspirations are quite refreshingly not always sensible. The priorities for our work may start with food, warmth, shelter and reproduction; but grandiose and often seemingly pointless schemes consume just as much passion, if not more. The building of cathedrals and monuments, the channel tunnel, putting man on the moon, great conquests of all sorts, exploration, scientific research, great literature and works of art – such aspirations may not satisfy any economic model, but are they always wrong? Not really: such work constructively engages human hands and minds and is no different from what people do with their own lives. Pure efficiency (e.g., going solely for economic growth) is not actually an end in itself at all, and human beings need to be allowed sufficient expression to live their lives with variety and pleasure. The proposed new model allows individual corporations to have individual equity holders who can choose to pursue any aspiration they like for their company.

Trading cycles

Cycles are as natural, unpredictable and inevitable as the weather. For centuries, there was nothing so vital or so vulnerable as the annual harvest. That was what income savings were for, to compensate for the cycles and smooth them out.

How does the proposed model help us to deal with such cycles? Firstly, there is, as explained previously, the inbuilt flexibility for participators to reduce their immediate cash payments in return for rewards later (through equity units). Secondly, the model gives less emphasis to residual income being a return on capital, and instead regards it as the source of creating true independence and maturity, true integrity for the objectives of the company: the capacity to constantly re-invest for the future – in a secure capital base, in modern technology, and in education and training. Only really *spare* surplus profits are likely to be distributed to be spent for pleasure. The model has a built-in bias to limit cash distributions (to equity holders) to those sums, the payment of which would not jeopardise the corporation's capital funding needs.

International implications

There should be no impact on the ability of UK companies or individuals to invest in those overseas corporations that operate according to more traditional 'capitalist' lines. Where corporations invest abroad, the usual fiscal rules about transfer pricing (i.e., having inter-corporation pricing that does not distort the profits attributable to the proper entity) are likely to continue to apply as they do today.

Similarly, there is nothing to stop overseas individuals or companies participating in UK corporations as they do under existing rules. They can contribute in any form as equity participators, just as UK-based companies and individuals can. The most common such participation is likely to be capital investment, and the most obvious change for such investors is that the capital market for that product, insofar as it is risk capital, will be somewhat more lively (reflecting the fact that risk capital will be more frequently recycled than it is today). If a UK company has some overseas equity unit holders, but also some here in the UK (and one assumes that this is bound to include some of the workforce and directors), then at least a portion of the corporate tax will be paid to the UK. Moreover, the proposed new model can comfortably co-exist with the existing traditional form of corporation as well.

No particular difficulty is foreseen in relation to the new form of corporation competing with overseas companies. The anticipated smaller size of most of the new form of corporation (i.e., not having elaborate consolidated structures with wholly-owned subsidiaries) is not likely to be an issue, as in those trades where size is important – such as oil exploration, or major infrastructure projects – the new corporations will still have an incentive to be large enough in themselves to compete internationally.

The taxation of foreign corporations is a major problem today, where some companies base their head office in low-tax jurisdictions and thereby avoid taxation in those other countries where they do in fact have a large market. This means that they can earn substantial profits from the population of another country without paying much tax in that country. How would the proposed new corporate model work in relation to this problem?

If the foreign corporation trades in the UK as an outsider (i.e., as a foreign company and not as a new-style corporation) then its taxation position would be as it is today. It would of course be unable to offer its core staff or other participators in the UK any equity units, as it wouldn't have any. It would then have to compete with UK companies that did. That should mean that it would find it harder to compete: there would be market pressure for it to offer equity units.

If the foreign corporation did offer equity units, then core employees and other participators would benefit in precisely the same way that they would from UK corporations. The fact that the new corporation was based abroad could mean that it only paid tax abroad, but an interesting point arises, and it is this. Should the corporate tax be due in the country where the head office or registered office is based, or should such corporate tax be apportioned between those countries according to where the current equity unit holders live? The latter choice would be the more logical, as then those enterprises that require much participation from contributors in another country would pay more of its tax there. We can, of course, hardly complain if those corporations that merely bought services in from the UK market and resold to it (without granting equity units to any participators in the UK) paid no tax here, as no one here has done anything to earn tax for the UK. All the enterprise, and all the participation, has been abroad. That is what competition is all about. It is up to a UK based company to offer competing services – but at least without the distorting hindrance of sales taxes like VAT or payroll taxes like income tax/national insurance making it harder.

Charities
How would the proposed model of the corporation apply to 'not-for-profit' companies, which might otherwise wish to use the existing limited company model, usually adapted by being limited by guarantee?

An incorporated charity would have equity units just like any other new corporation, but if the organisation is to qualify as a properly-registered charity (such as under the present UK Charity Commission provisions), then it follows that not only does it have to declare its objects to be exclusively charitable, but it also has to accept an absolute prohibition on the distribution of profits or capital to any of its unit holders. How can that be achieved? Simply by declaring that the units give control but carry no monetary rights either to capital or to residual profits. The corporation's constitution will set out clearly, such as under the historic 'objects clause' of the Memorandum of Association, the aims and objects to which the charity's operational efforts are directed, and any surplus funds will have to be applied either to those specific objects or to another registered charity with objects as close to those as possible.

In a similar way, the existing practice of having a wholly-owned 'trading subsidiary', to allow a charity to reap the benefits of commercial trading without compromising the charitable operations and status of the main entity, can still apply. Another corporation may be formed with equity units issued as usual, but again with a prohibition on these carrying any monetary rights, because in this case, the declared objects will be solely the support of the originating charity. Thus the trading subsidiary may be effectively exempted from corporation tax (as it is today) on the strict condition that it covenants to (and does) donate, on a permanent basis, any and all surplus funds representing residual profits to a registered charity as its originating charity, while in all other respects operating as a commercial corporation in its contractual arrangements.

There is much to be said for a very thorough review of the whole of charity legislation in the UK, even to give consideration as to whether charities as presently conceived are relevant at all. But that is a wholly different subject to what we are concerned about here.

10 Limited liability revisited

What happens when losses are made?
Much has been written earlier in this book about what should happen to the profits or surpluses made by a corporation, and to whom they are attributable. But what happens if the corporation makes a loss? Obviously a small loss is simply a negative profit, and so is deducted from other profits made; but what happens if the loss is substantial – so much so that it exceeds the company's reserves? These reserves comprise all the company's accumulated profits to date, to the extent that they have not yet been paid out. 'Reserves' however also include what is currently known as 'share capital'. Shareholders (or under our proposed new model, risk capital providers) have agreed to put their capital at risk of loss: that is precisely what risk capital is. So catastrophic losses will devour both accumulated profits and the subscribed risk capital. But who should bear the cost of losses after that? That is the subject of this chapter.

Under the existing model of the corporation, the equity shareholders of a limited company have 'limited liability', which means that their liability in the event of catastrophic loss is limited to what they have paid (or are due to pay) into the company for their shares. As their liability is *limited,* the unpaid creditors of the company cannot demand any more from them than what they have already invested. This made sense when the corporate model worked in the way it did, so that shareholders (with little day-to-day control over a company's affairs) parted with fixed sums of investment and left it to the directors to make something out of it. But under our proposed new model of the corporation, there is supposed to be much closer monitoring of the company's performance by the equity unit holders in conjunction with the directors. Moreover, with the broadening of the concept of equity to extend beyond the provision of capital, we should perhaps re-visit the whole question of limited liability. Should this protect just capital providers, or all participators? Should it exist at all? Indeed it is something of an absurdity that those at the heart of the entity – those in control of it and receiving all its profits – should be protected, while everyone else is exposed to the cost of their failure (assuming the losses can be blamed on those in charge). To what extent are the equity unit holders, or indeed the directors, responsible for such losses?

At the heart of this debate, two separate issues can be distinguished: firstly, to what extent are the equity unit holders, or indeed the directors, actually *responsible* for such losses? And secondly, there is the practical issue of whether it actually does any good (i.e., whether it actually helps economic activity generally) to pursue the individuals concerned for such responsibility.

The practical implications of unlimited liability are profound. The principal argument in favour of unlimited liability centres on the matter of *blame* or responsibility, whereas the principal arguments against it are more pragmatic and concern the likely practical outcomes.

The causes of loss
It is difficult to find much reliable evidence of the underlying causes of corporate insolvency, but surveys of the causes of failure by commercial agencies highlight two main classes: causes for which the management of the failing concern may be held responsible, and causes attributable to external factors over which the business can exercise little or no control. Generally, causes in the first category (including insufficient resources, management failings, poor cost control, inadequate planning – more competition than expected, insufficient margins, insufficient demand, etc.) are thought to amount to the great majority, possibly as high as 75% or even 80% of all insolvencies. Causes in the second category (including natural disasters, totally unexpected competition or highly unlikely failures of other concerns) make up the rest.

In circumstances where *external* factors have caused the failure of a corporation, and little or no blame attaches to the directors or equity holders, then it could be argued that those persons should not bear losses for which they have not been responsible. The argument against this is simple: those persons would have enjoyed the *profits* whether these were carefully planned or a windfall: if sharing in profits does not require evidence of direct responsibility, but is as of right, then why should losses not be treated the same way? Of course, all who engage in economic activity are aware of the risks involved. But if there are to be certain circumstances in which equity holders are *not* to be held liable for losses, the problem becomes one of *who* is to make the decision regarding the main cause of failure, and what rights of appeal do the protagonists have? That way lies a minefield.

Let us now look at circumstances where management are likely to be held responsible. For the present, let us not distinguish between the organisational input of directors from that of the equity holders: essentially, they share the task. Together they give the corporation its vision and its identity: when they work together as a cohesive and enthusiastic team, planning and executing bold but soundly-reasoned decisions, then the results should be successful. Assuming for a moment that there are no destructive external influences, then if the results are *not* successful, it is hard to see who else *other* than the equity holders together with the directors can possibly be responsible for any losses arising from failings of planning, management or control. It is the effectiveness and sheer competence of the teamwork function in planning, guiding, controlling and motivating the corporation that is the major factor in achieving profits, and therefore the major factor causing any losses. That is the argument.

Let us briefly look a little deeper into the detailed causes of loss due to management failings. Here is a selection of possible causes:

- Inadequate awareness of business circumstances, poor financial or control systems

- Inadequate initial capital, or loss or subsequent destruction of capital assets, excessive commitments or under-insurance

- Inadequate sales, bad debts from existing sales, inadequate 'added value' (trading margins) to justify fixed expenditure, or some other structural weakness including unforeseen external factors which could realistically have been provided for

- Excess or inappropriate expenditure for the level of sales achievable

- Continuing to trade in an unrealistic resistance to the inevitable decline of a particular niche or type of operation.

In the proposed model, it is the equity unit holders who decide on the commercial 'niche' for the company, agree the budget (even if they do not actually set it), and who, in an ultimate sense, appoint and supervise the directors in their monitoring of corporate activity, and it is the directors who take responsibility for the detailed implementation of all those plans.

It does seem as though, at every level, the corporation's failure (if other than from totally unexpected and unforeseeable outside events, which must be rare) can be attributable either to lack of planning or foresight in relation to conditions outside the corporation, or to failings or misjudgements in the initial plan, subsequent plans, implementation, or general or detailed management, all of which must, strictly speaking, be related back to the duty of the equity holders and the directors, who between them set the course and control the whole enterprise. Indeed a well-run organisation should be able to plan and prepare for most of the *unexpected* outside events: identifying all the potential threats in advance; holding back sufficient reserves for all sorts of contingencies; watching major customers carefully for signs of insolvency; insuring for all possible risks; systematically shrinking an operation that clearly is declining, and so on. There are extremely few genuinely unforeseeable catastrophes. Logically, in terms of fair responsibility, one might therefore conclude that a corporation's losses are attributable to the equity unit holders, in conjunction with the directors – who are, of course, likely to be among the equity unit holders anyway. This argument is quite separate from the straightforward conclusion that those who enjoy the profits should also bear the losses.

What happens with limited liability?

The amount of share capital and the existence of undistributed reserves are together intended to represent the full amount of cushioning needed against potential loss. If a corporation has sufficient reserves to support its business plan, then there should be adequate protection against the corporation becoming insolvent.

Unfortunately in practice, most business failures seem to result not only in the shareholders losing their capital, but also in the non-payment of ordinary business suppliers, i.e., the unsecured creditors. In fact the bad trading debts which arise as a result can then in turn be the cause of failure for the supplying companies, and the cycle can then accelerate, as economic uncertainty reduces security values and thereby banking facilities, and squeezes normal payment cycles by reducing accommodation allowed on trust.

This happens because under present insolvency rules for limited companies in the UK, any losses that exceed reserves and share capital are then borne fully and directly by the unsecured creditors, who are usually those ordinary trading suppliers who just happen to have been caught as being the latest suppliers to the company.

It is a feature of the closing stages just before insolvency that whether or not you are one of those who get paid can be entirely arbitrary and capricious. Suppliers may get paid in full up till June, but if you unwittingly continued to supply in July, you lose out entirely, as far as that July bill is concerned. There are regulations governing the very last payments of an insolvent company, which aim to recover some of these payments and spread them out for the benefit of all the unpaid creditors. These regulations are occasionally resorted to (provided the liquidator has sufficient funds available to do so), but tend to catch only the most obvious cases of preferential payment. In any event, the question of preferential payments only arises when some debts incurred in one month (for example) have been paid in full, while others incurred in the same month have not, and, to that extent, together with the very high costs of a formal winding-up, have the effect of levelling down payments to creditors rather than levelling up.

The test of unfairness – and therefore whether or not the law interferes as far as this particular provision is concerned – is solely concerned with preference in terms of date (e.g., the intention to see a favourite creditor paid for his supplies in July while others in that month remain unpaid), rather than preference in terms of category of debt. If everybody who supplied goods in June is paid in full, and nobody who supplied goods in July or later gets anything, then that is deemed to be entirely fair and proper, and the present law will only interfere, by possibly seeking a contribution from the directors, if the directors were positively 'wrongful' to have continued to trade beyond June. Whether or not the sword of Damocles falls upon a particular supplier can therefore depend on something as random as the date of supply, and what is most distressing is that this feature will probably have been quite incidental to that supplier.

Let's face it, *somebody* has to lose out in every insolvency. Under the present system, the ones who are hit worst are those nearest to the tree when it falls, regardless of what awareness or responsibility they may have had, if any, for holding it up or cutting it down. That would seem to be plainly inequitable. Moreover, this has the effect that, as soon as there is any whiff of insolvency, everybody in the know keeps well away. Trade credit in particular tends to dry up, quite understandably. That surely cannot be in the best interests of the corporation.

That, in short, is how the current system of limited liability works: those who did not share in profits (and who almost certainly had no responsibility for the losses) lose out, while those who did share in profits, and who probably had full responsibility for the losses, are protected. How can we have arrived at such an absurd situation?

Historically, limited liability was devised for the benefit of a single class of participator – the capital provider – to the detriment, if necessary, of all the others. We have indicated above who are most likely to be responsible for heavy losses: the equity holders and the directors. In the present model, it is precisely and solely these persons who are protected. Everybody else has *unlimited* liability. [The directors have no automatic liability, unless a specific and costly legal action can be successfully mounted to show conclusively that they acted wrongly (and that means recklessly rather than merely incompetently) or fraudulently. These instances are extremely rare in comparison to the number of insolvencies in which ordinary trading suppliers suffer loss.] So who does lose out? Usually the most innocent and uninvolved parties of all – those supplying goods or services in good faith, on credit, with (usually) no interest charge and no security. The problem is compounded by the fact that even the costs of winding-up an insolvent company, supposedly formed for their own benefit by the capital-providers, who have now shrugged their shoulders and walked away, is left to be effectively paid by those suppliers unfortunate enough to not get paid in full by the company.

That, in simple terms, is the present system.

Who *exactly* should have unlimited liability?

By definition, in a corporate insolvency, someone is bound to lose out: earlier we came to the logical conclusion that this should be the group of those ultimately responsible for the corporation's overall direction. This could be either the directors or the equity unit holders, or some or all of both of them.

Let us consider the principles underlying how we might reach a conclusion on this. Firstly, bearing in mind the magnitude of what is at stake, we need a determination that is unambiguous: there must be no room for dispute over whether a party is or is not liable. Secondly, those responsible must have clearly accepted their responsibility knowingly and willingly. And finally, it must be *just* and *fair*, i.e., those responsible must have not only enjoyed the profits of trading but also have had the authority to control the way in which the corporation was directed and managed: in other words, they must have been in a position to do something about the way the company was run and ended up insolvent.

There is a case for suggesting that the equity unit holders exercise collective 'cabinet' responsibility, together with the directors, for all their decisions, leading to the suggestion that every member of both boards is equally liable. But this does not entirely satisfy the principles we have just outlined above: a single director may have been appointed for a specific contribution and accordingly would refuse to act if she knew that she would become personally liable for the corporation's failure; as a specialist, she may indeed be ill-equipped to exercise overall control.

If we start at the beginning, the corporation's initial directors – who hold all the equity units at that stage – will be liable for losses as there is no one else. When they then offer equity units to others, such as risk capital providers, they can then include either full or partial liability in the terms of that issue of units. Some investors may provide capital at a late stage to avert insolvency, requiring equity units as a reward (but not a directorship as they do not want to get involved in management): it would seem unjust to make such persons personally liable for losses. Similarly, there may be additional directors who are more in the nature of 'salaried partners' than 'equity partners', and who therefore do not hold equity units and could reasonably decline to accept liability. That again is reasonable. One comes to the conclusion that the only arrangement that fits all the principles we outlined earlier is that the full exposure to liability should be borne by those individuals who are *both* directors *and* equity unit holders.

It is a very compelling argument that those individuals who not only share in the control of the corporation and in its profits, but also have joint responsibility for its management and direction, should be the ones to bear the cost of its failure. Having said that, it is possible that a minority of these individuals could specify (in their contractual agreement) some limit to that exposure. This might particularly apply to the unit holders/directors of the largest corporations with strong reserves, where there is a case to be made for personal liability to be (publicly) restricted to some specific limit, leaving those dealing with the company to be aware of the risk they are taking. This makes sense when the amount of the individuals' resources is insignificant in comparison to the potential liabilities.

As far as those few occasions are concerned where the corporation's failure is entirely due to external causes beyond reasonable foresight, there could be provisions limiting the liability of those who are both directors and equity unit holders, although one must acknowledge that it is just as inequitable in such circumstances for the unsecured creditors to suffer loss.

The implications of unlimited liability

It is one thing to argue for unlimited liability on the grounds of logical responsibility, but what exactly are the practical advantages of doing this?

1 Unlimited liability encourages a greater and more active interest generally on the part of those individuals in ultimate control of the corporation. It provides real meaning for equity participation. Key equity unit holders who are also directors are more likely to properly supervise and monitor all that is going on.

2 It motivates the board and equity holders to be more forward-thinking, and call the earliest possible meeting to discuss the position whenever there is a potential future risk of insolvency.

This achieves one of two things. Either the corporation immediately ceases to trade (or the undertaking is successfully sold as a going concern to fresh equity holders), so that losses generally are at a minimum, or else continuation proposals are put forward. In the latter eventuality, if the long-term prospects are poor but the current trading is satisfactory, then there can be a gradual, managed slimming down of the operation, rather than blindly soldiering on. If matters are more serious, but not desperate, then this will probably involve there being changes among the unit holders, requiring either (a) that a satisfactorily sustainable plan, which avoids risk of loss, can be implemented, or (b) that the body of unit holders themselves agree to attenuate their contractual requirements for the time being to a level at which a sustainable plan becomes possible. This contrasts with the present motivation whereby we have some shareholders and directors who give up too readily (and waste all that the business has achieved) after pressure from bankers and dark hints about insolvent trading, and we have other quite different shareholders and directors who, often at little further risk to themselves, keep a company blindly staggering on with only the slimmest chance of avoiding failure. The rules were tightened considerably by the Insolvency Act 1986 but, even so, there is a large gap between the reasonable decisions of an ordinary person having *automatic* personal responsibility for failure and the potential risks of some responsibility following a successful action in an offence of wrongful trading.

3   There is a little more incentive for suppliers to continue to support the corporation by continuing to give credit in difficult times, contrary to the motivation under existing rules. If creditors know that they are more likely get paid in the end, then they are less troubled about extending credit to potentially insolvent corporations. In such circumstances, they can be offered short-term equity units (without a directorship) at that stage. One of the most detested features of insolvency today, is the sudden and unexpected cliff edge for the suppliers – the instant transition from payment in full to nothing at all. Paradoxically, the confidence of suppliers is actually enhanced if there is *less* confidentiality about a corporation's difficult financial position – something rendered more possible if the

corporation has access to additional reserve funds from the pool of equity holders/directors and has the facility to offer a short-term share in the equity.

4   It encourages corporations to ensure that they have sufficient risk capital, and to *save* so as to make themselves financially independent and to have adequate resources for all future possibilities. The propensity to spend next year's earnings for this year's satisfaction is a root cause of the inability of many businesses, and individuals, to survive temporary setbacks and recessions, because it tends to completely close off the vital options of being able to make fundamental and costly, but necessary, changes, or to trade successfully at a lower level than the optimum preferred. At present, there is an incentive for the directors of public companies to declare and pay higher dividends than perhaps they should, hoping that this will encourage share prices to rise. By this means, the company benefits from the status and positive press coverage that higher share prices give; those holding share options will also benefit from a boost in share prices; but the company's reserves are depleted.

Unlimited liability does of course ignore the practical problems of recovery from equity unit holders/directors, which in turn depends on their resources, and this is addressed later in this chapter; but often the mere prospect of real personal liability achieves an improvement in the adequacy of financial reserves, the extent of concern and the quality of decision-making. Such a proposal will emphasise the need for unit holders to obtain regular assurances from the directors that all foreseeable disaster risks have adequate insurance cover; and will reinforce the urgency for sound and independent financial reporting. It must be said that most insolvencies are of the smaller companies, for whom these provisions are paramount; unlimited liability for directors/equity holders of larger public companies may be regarded as unrealistic, but again it is probably the threat (and change in attitude) that is most important, and besides, such insolvencies are rare.

In recent years there has been a groundswell of reaction against high-geared (leveraged) corporations, such that in the debt-equity debate, current opinion strongly favours *equity* funding rather than *debt* funding. What precisely does this mean? It means that there is a preference for corporations to have their risk capital provided by persons who are only paid if the corporation makes a profit, and whose capital is only repaid if the corporation is able to pay all of its other debts. But, again, what does this really mean? Surely what it says, is that if a corporation fails, then it is better that the cost of failure be borne by the shareholders (i.e., the equity unit holders in our proposed model) than by the general body of creditors. And that is what unlimited liability provides – whatever the apparent gearing (or leverage) is.

Practical considerations: the case against unlimited liability
There are a number of objections to the argument for unlimited liability, although these are principally on practical grounds. Some of these might be identified as follows:

1 It would make it harder to raise large sums of equity capital from lots of small investors if the individuals are going to be personally liable for corporate losses. While investors are happy to place specified amounts at risk, they are far less prepared to expose themselves to unquantifiable risks beyond the sum concerned. This may tend to lead to a reduction in the amount of risk capital investment that would be made available. However, this objection only applies to those investors who are appointed as directors as well.

2 Some people who would otherwise make valuable and effective participators and directors may be deterred by the prospect of unlimited liability.

3 There could be an element of unfairness between participators whose resources vary, as wealthier ones are more likely to be pursued for the greater part of any shortfall, regardless of how few equity units they hold.

4 It would be naive to think that there would not be any difficulties in pursuing equity holders personally, and in identifying and realising sufficient of their assets. In smaller enterprises, the participators will already have invested all they have; in larger ones, those involved are bound to protect their most valuable

assets in family trusts. In practice, therefore, recoveries from equity holders may yield very little.

5   The fear of personal liability may reduce the boldness of managerial decisions and lead to the selection of some very tame and colourless boards of directors, such that the quality of corporate enterprise might suffer a material decline.

6   In the bigger picture, it could be considered a retrograde step for corporate insolvency to result additionally in the undignified pursuit into bankruptcy of the equity holders/directors as well, regardless of individual blame. Limited liability has been the spur to encourage huge amounts of venture capital to be placed at high risk in many commercial enterprises, to the great benefit (overall) of many of those involved. In some industries, there can be serial failures until one of the companies finally gets it right: is that something to be promoted or discouraged?

7   There is no *real* evidence that much would change: after all, sole traders and partnerships (with unlimited liability) fail regularly as well.

We shall now try to respond to these objections.

Those responsible for corporate funding provided by large institutions – and this means all the 'blue chip' investments of pension funds and the like – would not want to expose themselves (or their employers) to any risk of unlimited liability, and so would almost certainly decide not to seek appointment as a director of any corporation in which they invested. That is of course no different from their approach at the present time. In any event, we saw in Chapter 4 that much of corporate equity funding was not in the nature of true risk capital at all. These institutions are free to choose between proper participatory funding (involving a directorship together with all that that entails), plain equity funding, or simply making loan capital available. Equity funding (without a directorship) does offer the opportunity for some involvement through monthly meetings, as well as a reward equivalent to present equity shares. The provision of loan capital (as opposed to equity capital) without any influence over the corporation would still offer the investor a reasonable rate of interest (suitable for unsecured loans) and even the potential for some further contractual supplement, without any risk of liability.

This would mean that those institutions that presently invest in equity shares would still have as many opportunities open to them as they do at present, without being at any risk of unlimited liability if severe losses were made. Similar considerations might apply to the 'rich uncle' type of loan, because if an investor expressly does not want any responsibility in managing the company, then there is no sense in his being appointed as a director: if he *does* want this in addition to his part ownership of the equity of the company, then he will become liable for any losses. True equity participators would deserve their reward, and market pressures would, one imagines, always ensure that such individuals (those having control and management and so taking all the real risks) would be well chosen.

It is inevitable that this proposal will expose the disinterest of many existing investor directors in established corporations. That in turn may possibly drive downwards the perceived value of the contribution that both pure capital and pure 'salaried' directorships make to economic activity. The provision of capital without further risk or effort or commitment cannot truly be said to be proper equity participation at all. Idle spare wealth without accompanying enterprise, effort, or organisational supervision (i.e., pure capital as a contribution on its own) probably has less economic value than the present corporate model provides: it is for the market to determine the answer to this question – and, at last, capitalism itself will be exposed to market forces! Let's be honest: there is a world of difference between a creator of or true participant in economic activity, and someone simply looking for an effortless home for dormant wealth.

It does not in fact follow that, just because the return is lower, less capital will be made available, even if the reduction in returns is universal. The true effect depends on the returns available from competing applications – the laws of supply and demand – and, as was seen earlier in this book, the returns available to idle investment in bank deposits depends in turn upon the productive use to which they can be put.

There are, of course, a number of specific solutions available to the issue of unlimited liability. Those directors with personal liability will want to spread that risk as much as possible. One way for them to do this is to make an offer of equity units to other participators, specifying the amount of additional resources which are to be committed in support of the feature of unlimited liability, so that the individual equity holder may declare a specific sum which represents the maximum extent of his exposure. [This would be acceptable so long as there are others who continue to have unlimited liability.] It is then for the directors, if they wish, to verify that he or she has these assets available, but in any event, it is likely that such new equity holders will either try to exclude their domestic home (for example) or at least specify only what they can really afford to lose. That way, the position for new equity-holding directors could be conveniently managed until the individual became better acquainted with the company's circumstances.

It would always be for market forces to determine, in the light of adequate knowledge, the extent to which the market is prepared to deal with a corporation to which the participators offer only limited reserve assets. By enabling suppliers and other outsiders to take a considered view of the depth or shallowness of the equity pool, the new corporation then puts these unsecured creditors in almost as knowledgeable a position as bankers! To achieve this disclosure properly the directors would of course have to regularly publish an updated list of equity holders and their committed resources, but only if these are being restricted in some way.

It is not altogether unreasonable to require that only *some* of the equity holders/ directors should have unlimited liability. To consider this more carefully, let us go back to the starting point. The promoters form the corporation and create the initial equity. These promoters then become the initial directors/equity holders and take the corporation forward; at this point they bear all the risks and take all the reward. But then they invite others to join them as participators, others who will increase the corporation's equity value but also acquire the right to a portion of it. Some of these new equity holders may be less keen to assume fully unlimited liability. Fine: it just means that the directors have only been able to off-load *some* of their burden upon others.

What matters is that the original directors and some of their successors (presumably those who will be significant equity holders) are then left *by default* with unlimited liability – so that the ultimate back-stop in insolvency is that those who actually started the company and their true participating successors are the ones to bear the cost personally. Similarly, if the company is in some difficulty, critical suppliers to the company who are concerned about payment of their account may take a small amount of equity units to provide them with some control and some eventual compensation: these participators in particular will want limited liability, and could perfectly fairly be given that (they simply avoid being directors of that company as well).

It is envisaged that the recovery from a unit holder should be proportional to the number of his units. If we assume that the workforce has some representative on the board of directors as well as holding equity units, then it may be that they could transfer their equity units into some sort of union fund, whereupon there might be some freedom from immediate personal risk of loss as well. In the case of large employers, the institutions managing such funds might be able to provide or arrange professional representatives to sit on the board of governors, and this should provide additional protection for the employees concerned.

We can now see that there are effective and workable solutions available to answer the objections under (1), (2), (3) and (4). This just leaves us to deal with the objections under (5), (6) and (7).

Objection (5), concerning the reduced incentive to make bold decisions, is perhaps more perceived than real – perceived, that is, by persons who have never engaged in the sharp end of business themselves. In very few small limited companies do the directors at present find themselves entirely free from personal liability. In the majority of cases, the directors (who are usually also the shareholders) have to guarantee the bank borrowings and, if the company occupies leasehold premises, the full terms of the lease as well. The result is that the failure of the company will usually lead to the bank calling upon the guarantee, which in turn is usually supported by a charge over the director's family home. For such businesses, therefore, the director's very home is directly 'on the line'. Does that lead to timid decisions in small businesses?

If a proper survey were to be made of small companies, the empirical evidence would probably suggest that unlimited liability has no detrimental effect on the boldness of board decisions. Certainly, anecdotal experience suggests that small businessmen with personal guarantees hovering over them display as much colour and enterprise – and profitability – as any other. By contrast, the very real doubt over recovering trading debts from other limited companies as *customers* is a more serious obstacle to business confidence. If these doubts were removed by making the key equity-holding groups personally liable, then there would be more likelihood of positive growth in sales, fewer unexpected bad debts and more economic health generally. The two greatest concerns routinely expressed by small businesses are slow payment by customers and bad debts among them.

It was only very recently that professional firms of solicitors or accountants could protect themselves by means of a Limited Liability Partnership (LLP). Exposure to the risk of unlimited liability for the previous century did not appear to be a major obstacle to the calibre of candidates for admission to equity partnership in such firms (possibly compensated for by the opportunity to earn substantial profits), although clearly when the opportunity to have limited liability arose, it was taken advantage of. What happened was largely a reaction to the awarding of substantial litigation damages (in professional negligence claims, particularly in the USA) where these exceed existing insurance cover: the problem here probably lies more in the unreasonableness of the quantum of the litigation compensation than in the fact of unlimited liability.

Similarly, for many centuries Lloyds Names, i.e., the underwriters for some of the world's greatest potential insured disasters, were personally liable for claims without limit; some went bankrupt in the difficult days of the early 1990s. It is difficult to imagine exposure to greater risks, yet there was no shortage of candidates preparing to stand as Names. Again, obviously, this was compensated for by the prospect of considerable gain.

Clearly those involved in the control and direction of corporations have to be bold and competent. If they cannot at the same time handle other people's wealth with the same care with which they handle their own, then they should not be appointed to the job. They are, after all, being allowed a major stake in the corporation's net worth in return for their work and commitment. The anticipated resistance, in the case of larger companies in particular, is likely to reflect their poor confidence in organisational effectiveness, which is either that they do not have sufficient control from top to bottom to ensure that proper protection, as demanded from the top, is in place, or else that the individual departments at the bottom (i.e., at the interface with the market) are not sufficiently trained or self-motivated to be aware of the risks being engaged in, and as a result, do not themselves seek to systematically eliminate or avoid such risks.

In both cases the ultimate fault lies, arguably, with the directors/equity holders themselves.

What can we say about the undignified prospect of individual bankruptcies mentioned in objection (6)? Insolvency, generally, is an undignified and unwelcome event for all those involved. When it is inevitable, then there is little that can be done to avoid it. The answer is, firstly, to build into the system an incentive upon all those able to influence events, which will drive them as far as possible to avoid insolvency. This is more likely to be achieved with unlimited liability in the proposed model than with the existing one. Secondly, if insolvency does have to happen, then we must try to ensure that the inevitable cost, and the indignity, will fall where it is most equitable. Its effect should not be arbitrary or capricious. Thirdly, there is a case to be made for personal 'bankruptcy' to be brought into the twenty-first century: perhaps a person's private home up to a modest value (such as 60% of the average house price in that area) and a modest car, etc., could be exempt from being possessed – while investments recently transferred into trust funds or their spouse's name would be caught. The aim is not to punish or destroy failed businessmen, merely to collect assets that should be available to creditors. The whole procedure could be much swifter, cheaper, and more effective than it is at present.

In comparing the existing rules to those of the proposed scheme with unlimited liability, we are in effect weighing the present burden of loss, which often falls somewhat arbitrarily on the least involved (in the sense of their being both least aware and least responsible for the loss), namely the least pushing and the most recent suppliers, against the proposed burden which would fall on those who are most likely to have known exactly what was happening and were best placed to take remedial action. The argument, on the basis of principle rather than pragmatism, does make a compelling case. And if there is to be any indignity, it is better that it should apply to those responsible for causing it.

Finally, in response to objection (7), we have to admit that sole traders and small (unlimited) partnerships do indeed fail, but one has to remember that these are the smallest, most vulnerable, often least experienced, and possibly least professionally-organised businesses in the UK. They are not typical of the *average* business, and hardly comparable to the medium or large corporation. Many of the new, untried business ventures (of which as many as half fail within the first three years) do in fact start off in the form of sole traders and partnerships. Finally, many of these small, unincorporated businesses never had the chance to raise adequate risk capital in the first place. In the light of these facts, it is no surprise that so many unincorporated businesses should fail, and the fact that they do is not valid evidence of the impact unlimited liability would have on the average corporation.

Review of the situation

What effect are these proposals for unlimited liability likely to have on parties who would be interested in a directorship and a share in the equity units? Casual punters looking for a quick profit are likely to be deterred. Capital providers disinterested in exercising any control function will avoid directorships but may still be interested in the monthly meetings, or else they might provide instead long-term unsecured loans with reasonable rates of interest but without equity participation (as discussed above). Institutional capital providers, those keen to still enjoy equity participation, will be unaffected (as they are not generally on the board of directors), although they may well arrange professional governors to attend the monthly meetings to safeguard their investment and their reputation.

Employees will be as keen as ever to have equity units, although if any of them are directors as well, then they may insist in restricting their liability, as noted above; in any event, they will share the desire to see firm control exercised at all times. In such circumstances, such 'worker directors' would share a tremendous pressure for the workforce to be realistic in wage demands, as well as to hold down dividend payments, and to ensure the efficient and profitable operation of their company. [Is that such a bad outcome?] Their risk of financial loss would, one hopes, be balanced by what must be in practice a greater prospect of job security. In general, all equity holders will want to know that there is adequate risk capital in place, and the prodigal distribution of reserves will be eliminated. Suppliers, if their role is significant, will probably still want some participation if it is offered, provided that the company is well-managed and they are not required as directors as well; but their desire for equity units may be tempered by their reluctance to play an effective supervisory role.

If the company is already insolvent and there are no satisfactory plans for an early return to solvency, then no one will want units, and the corporation is best closed down. If there are satisfactory plans for an early return to solvency, then there is no undue risk to the equity unit holders (but potential profit) provided that the directors are competent to put the plans into action. The attitude of suppliers will obviously depend on all these factors, but quite frankly, if they are prepared to act as directors, then if their potential exposure (as unit holders) is limited to, say, a third of their average annual payments, then the maximum loss is equivalent, broadly speaking, to four months supplies. In those circumstances, they may well prefer to support plans to keep the corporation going so as to achieve several more months of supplies, depending, of course, on the relation between the sums recoverable from the unit holders and the likely deficiency faced by creditors. On the credit side, the equity unit-months held at this stage could prove to be very remunerative. Above all, the unit holders will insist on exercising positive control over the corporation's affairs, to the benefit of all.

The general concept of limited liability as it applies to traditional companies today is argued to have a flawed basis, both in theory and in practice, viewed from any perspective other than that of the equity capital provider. Far from being a stimulant to business, limited liability is considered to be a major cause of the failure of other well-run companies whose supplies, in good faith, have not been paid for.

Summary

In conclusion, one must say that a major loss is a *team failure* of those having collective responsibility for the control and direction of the corporation. Those holding a material amount of equity units and who are also directors of the same company, i.e., the individuals who reap the profits while having control of management and direction, simply cannot avoid being responsible for their company's failure. It is for the team to sort out who is responsible for what: some members may have contractually limited their liability, while others will be fully liable. Ultimately, then, the directors who are also equity unit holders must bear full responsibility as a team; it is they, more than anyone else, who had the power to influence the direction in which the corporation was moving – and it is extremely difficult to argue against the concept that the body of persons that ultimately plans the strategy for profit, that ultimately controls the corporation, and that ultimately reaps the reward for it all, is the body of persons most appropriate to bear the cost of losses arising through failures in those responsibilities, all of which were assumed knowingly and willingly.

The proposed model of the corporation sees a fundamental distinction between the market outside the corporation and the participators within it. It is the market outside that offers the corporation the opportunity to make a surplus within itself. If the corporation makes losses, these too should be borne *within* the corporation, and the external market should not be affected or penalised for failures within a particular corporation. The ideal might be to have some form of insurance available to unit holders to provide them with a safety net, possibly paid for out of a compulsory levy, rather similar to the way in which all motorised road users are compulsorily required to be covered by insurance protecting any external third party from harm that they may cause. It would of course rob the sanction of loss of some of its positive effects, and thus should perhaps only be available (as a safety net for partial assistance) in cases where the circumstances of the loss were quite beyond the control of the parties concerned; but even so, there would be valuable market pressure from the insurers themselves.

There are strong arguments on each side in this complex matter, and the practical implications are profound. Unlimited liability is not essential to the proposed model of the corporation. It does, however, fit in snugly with all the other aspects of the proposed corporate model in order to achieve the ideal dynamics that we seek for corporate activity as a whole, and is therefore to be recommended.

11 Equity units in practice: some details

The plan
As has been explained earlier in this book, the directors initially command the enterprise as its promoters. They have to, because there is no one else around at that stage. At this point they draw up some form of business plan to be distributed among the other potential participators, and it is this plan that forms the background to any subsequent contractual relationship. The publication of this plan, and its discussion with the participators, is effectively the first 'Annual General Meeting' or AGM of the new entity, to be followed by a further AGM in each succeeding year, in the same way as for present limited companies. The plan sets out all the usual points in a business plan: the substance of the proposed business and its products or services, broad details of market analysis or research, details of proposed management, premises, and workforce, preliminary financial projections including anticipated funding requirements, and so on. But it will also need to set out the approximate number of equity units intended to be made available over the first period of operation; similarly, it is at subsequent AGMs that the overall extent of the issue of equity units for the forthcoming year is decided. Changes to this plan, such as the emergency need to issue more units for any reason, will obviously affect all existing unit holders, and can therefore only reasonably be sanctioned at a further meeting of unit holders called for the purpose.

The directors/promoters then invite all the other participators to enter into a contractual relationship with the new corporation in the manner suggested in earlier chapters and, through the natural system of free bargaining, the equity units are shared out among those contributories. The directors will obviously try to keep a significant proportion of the units for themselves, as provided for in their plan, and will also be responsible for any stock of unissued units to prepare for unexpected eventualities. The directors can only issue units to themselves in accordance with the business plan agreed at the previous AGM. No issue of equity units can be made without the sanction of the equity holders (or governors acting for them). Unissued units do not belong to anyone – they do not exist until they are issued, and so accrue no profit.

It has to be the directors who issue and cancel equity units, as they are the persons at the heart of the enterprise and in day-to-day control of those commercial transactions which give rise to the need for equity unit bargaining; they do of course have to answer to the AGM for any material deviations from the previously agreed business plan each year. The directors therefore co-ordinate all the participators. This is little different to what happens in practice in virtually all existing companies at the present time, but without the opportunity to offer equity participation to a wider market.

Active and passive equity

Under the proposed scheme, the directors *issue* and *cancel* equity units. While they are 'active', equity units other than those relating to a capital contribution, are not openly saleable – as they can only be held by those actively contributing to the corporation at the present time. To have free saleability would destroy the very sense of issuing the units: they are issued to accompany a specific contribution or participation that is personal to the equity unit holder. There are circumstances in which such units could, however, be transferable (either subject to the directors' approval, or in accordance with the provisions of any contractual agreement between equity holders) if the unit-holder passes the responsibility for her contribution to someone who succeeds her and who then makes the self-same contribution.

Those units that relate to a capital contribution are different, simply because the participation that attaches to them is a fungible commodity: cash. If one participator investing risk capital wants to pass his interest on to another who is prepared to provide the same capital on precisely the same terms, then the corporation has no complaint, and the equity units may as well be transferable. This would even apply in a smaller, 'private' company, although here as at present the directors may wish to approve the person acquiring equity units, to ensure that the body of equity unit holders was able to continue working together. The sense of teamwork matters in a smaller company. Capital contributors in most companies would therefore be in a position to realise their investment at any time, subject to the terms of the unit holder agreement; in fact, there can be no objection in a public company to capital providers freely selling their equity units so long as the transferee is bound by the same conditions attaching to the investment. In that sense, there is no difference for capital providers from holding existing shares, cash being a fungible commodity, so long as the terms of investment are unaffected. Labour providers would have an agreement, possibly formulated by their trade union or some similar body, to come into effect when they left the company, so that there were arrangements in place to cover eventualities.

For the purpose of simplicity in illustration, we shall assume that equity units are to be issued to take effect from the first day of a month, and to be cancelled with effect from the last day of a month. Over the course of an accounting year – and the accounting year will of course end well before the next AGM so that there is adequate time to produce an account of the previous year's trading – there will be a number of equity units in issue, each for periods of multiples of a month. While equity units are issued and cancelled as occasion demands, the special contribution they represent is of course not forgotten, and part of the accounting process for the company will be to keep a record of the transactions in such units so that there is a permanent record of the past 'equity value' of any particular participator's efforts on behalf of the corporation. This is important, because it is then a simple calculation to identify the amount of profit or loss attributable to any particular participator who has held equity units at any time during the year. The sharing of profits by equity unit holders works in a very similar way to that which applies in a partnership, when a new partner shares in the profits for that part of the year starting when he joins until that part when he leaves (usually apportioned on a time basis if monthly accounts have not been prepared).

The active equity unit holders at any one time are intended to be solely those persons contributing to the company at the present time in some vital way. Once that contribution ceases, then in accordance with any contractual agreement entered into, those equity units will be cancelled (for ease of calculation, let us say with effect from the end of the month); the record, however, of their entitlement to share in a proportion of the residual profits of the company, for the relevant period, is retained. The units now become 'passive equity units', and they neither attract further income nor possess any further power of control. At some stage when the corporation's cash flow permits, payment, perhaps together with some accrued interest, will be made to those persons to repay them the additional contribution they have earned, subject to adjustment for any subsequent losses.

On this basis, the current *active* equity of a company will always be held by those whose present and continuing contribution to the company is greater than can be measured by the simple price paid for their goods or services supplied, and these same persons will be the ones controlling the board of directors and having the entitlement to share in current profits. Similarly, at any one point the pool of capital represented by the equity unit holders in total (i.e., both active *and* passive equity) will be the totality of the reserves of the company, being the investment, with accrued interest, of all the most recent contributors to the company, who will be paid out their share when funds permit.

It is suggested that the accounting period should be for twelve months, as for existing corporations. This is a practical period, which is a compromise between timeliness and adequate accuracy in financial reporting, and is ideal for other needs, such as taxation. The profit for the year is divided by the number of equity unit months in issue for the period, and allocated to the participators accordingly. But the allocation is at this stage only notional.

Distribution of surpluses

Setting aside for the present the possibility of trading losses, we now have a corporation which has been paying an agreed price for all its contributions (from the directors, the employees, and the suppliers), as well as paying basic interest to its capital providers, and has an accumulated surplus after all these outgoings. This surplus – the value added to the overall market by the corporation – can be identified precisely with the past and present equity holders through the record of equity unit months; but it cannot necessarily be paid out at this stage or for some while to come.

Why not? Because in the context of equity participation, *periodic profit is the wrong measure for assessing dividend pay-out*. The existing term 'distributable profit' in accountancy and company law is a complete misnomer from a practical point of view. Periodic profit is very much a man-made concept; it is not a real surplus so much as a notional surplus. Profit without equivalent cash surplus (i.e., unrealised profit) does not happen outside of accountancy – you don't pick fruit from a tree until it is ripe! Periodic profit is a notional and only sometimes accurate exercise to help in the interim monitoring and comparison of business results, and is not the proper basis for assessing or calculating dividend payments: it is like apportioning the ripening of a fruit into accounting periods unrelated to the practical reality of the seasons.

The desire to pay out the surplus profit to the equity holders must be balanced by the survival and independence needs of the corporation. As with existing limited companies, the persons controlling the company need to plan ahead each year, and assess the cash resources required for future trading. Only then can it be seen whether there is any possibility of a cash surplus being available for distribution.

To return to an analogy of nature, you do not plant a tree from a seed and expect to have a crop of fruit twelve months later. The tree has to grow and achieve sustainability before there is any distributable surplus. Similarly when investing in a relatively new corporation (through the medium of equity units) there is an implied, automatic acceptance that there is a long time horizon – as well as uncertainty – before receiving tangible rewards. It may be five, ten or twenty years before passive equity units are finally paid their notional share of profit and are finally deleted from the records. Any earlier payment may possibly damage the capital fabric of the corporation. A continual high level of reinvestment in the up-dating of plant and equipment, the maintenance of premises, staff training, etc., and in the gradual repayment of debt, is essential for the true financial strength and independence of the corporation, and the sustainability of its future earnings, indeed its continued service to the community; on a macro-economic scale, a high level of reinvestment is frequently cited by leading international authorities as the key to sustained economic growth.

Once established, of course, a corporation should have distributable cash surpluses in most years. At that point, the corporation will have some accumulated profits (ignoring again the possibility of losses). Whenever profits are finally paid out, they will go to redeem the *earliest* passive equity units first. As we have seen, the equity holders may change, but their contribution is recorded for later reward. On this basis, there will always be a pool of residual, accumulated equity profits that will be due to the most recent contributories. Their patience in awaiting their reward, which is part of the fundamental concept of equity participation, is what keeps the corporation going; but by identifying profits with equity unit months and thereby with individual participators, the system is far more accurate than the existing limited company system of cash dividend payments, by automatically rewarding investors rateably for the period of their investment. What it does further, however, is to link that reward to the true *internal* actual profitability of the corporation, not to the external market perceptions – whereby the most dramatic movements in stock prices can be in response to factors bearing little relationship to the real underlying performance of the individual company.

Other considerations

It would be working against the whole concept of the scheme if active equity units were to be freely marketable, other than in the case of those units accompanying the provision of capital or some similar contribution, where the obligation for this contribution can be transferred. On the other hand, there is no logical argument against the assignability of passive equity units, because when an employee's or supplier's contribution has ceased and he loses his active share of control, the unit-months held are relevant only for ultimate receipt of the anticipated share in profits. There might be some market for the purchase of these passive units so as to resolve the difficulties that might otherwise arise in cases of the death or bankruptcy of a former contributor. This market would have to deduct an appropriate discount to reflect the uncertainty and delay in the fact and date of final payment. Passive equity units are, of course, still at risk to future losses (if such losses are big enough) on the grounds that they constitute the very reserves of the corporation: fire and storm can still happen even at the point when the harvest becomes ripe, but not yet picked!

Consideration will need to be given to the building-in of some sort of interest factor on the pool of equity employed. This would help to balance the slightly conflicting interests of active and passive equity holders. It would reflect the cost of having the use of those funds from passive equity, with such interest being deducted before arriving at the current equity profit, thus rendering present residual profits more accurate as a result. This would also ensure that passive equity holders, those with no more say in the corporation – who might otherwise be kept waiting for twenty years for their payout, to the distinct advantage of current active unit holders – would not see their position unduly prejudiced; and it would provide some degree of balance against the notion that they need never be paid out.

Dissolution

'Equity' and 'reserves' are *real* concepts in the corporation. Equity units, however, are only *notional* concepts purely for accounting purposes in order to calculate the suitable rewards for participants' involvement. The current possessor of an equity unit cannot individually demand payment of his or her share of profits. The question of payment is a matter for the directors under the control of the general body of unit holders. Only when a majority of those fundamentally involved in the corporation (i.e., of all the unit holders) are agreed that it is in keeping with the best interests of the corporation, can any payments be made to equity holders.

The same requirement applies whenever the times comes to wind up the corporation: if and when the general body of equity unit holders decides that the corporation can no longer achieve its aim (or has already achieved it and has no further purpose), and that it is no longer able to serve the community and should therefore be dissolved, then the corporation can cease trading and commence winding up. In the course of that winding up, all creditors will be settled in full first before anything is available to pay unit holders. The unit holders, both active and passive, will then receive their arrears of accumulated reserves, starting with the oldest unpaid holders first.

If there is a surplus or deficiency at this stage, then whether this is a capital or a revenue surplus or deficit, it logically goes to swell or diminish the existing pool of reserves belonging to the active equity holders. A capital adjustment is different from a revenue adjustment in the sense that it will generally have arisen over a period greater than that in which it arises: it will reflect the resale value, rather than book value, of fixed plant, vehicles, freehold premises, stocks, work in progress, goodwill, etc., less costs of realisation and winding up. If the balance sheet had been routinely prepared on the basis of resale values, then this problem of capital/revenue distinction would not so readily arise.

It might seem to follow that, whether it is a positive or negative adjustment, a capital profit or loss should be reflected proportionately among all remaining equity holders, whether active or passive. Indeed, it could be argued that the adjustment should be extended further to encompass all former equity holders on grounds of fairness (over- or under-valuations, and the final costs of winding up, could be said to have arisen rateably since the commencement of the corporation), but this is out-weighed by the administrative complications which would result from such a re-opening of past records. Many potential beneficiaries may have died, gone bankrupt, or simply moved away. Moreover, the practical likelihood is that any significant variation between book values and resale or break-up values, and indeed the justification for benefiting or suffering from this, are both attributable to the most recent few years represented by the current pool of equity (active and passive). In our fruit tree analogy, it is the current *active* equity holders who, being entitled to the prospective fruits of the tree (or deciding that it is now dead!), are deciding instead to cut it down and sell the stock of capital as timber. The active unit holders in all previous periods must be presumed to have had precisely the same opportunity to make this decision in their own circumstances, and from this it could be argued that the surplus or deficit, whether of a capital or revenue nature, should be apportioned among only the current active equity unit holders only.

Conclusion

This chapter has explained some of the detailed workings of the proposed model in order to illustrate its practicality. Clearly the detailed rules would need considerably more time and thought before being capable of being put into practice, but they can be seen to provide a reasonable guidance as to the workability of the model. Sufficient body has also been provided to enable the reader to assess the likely dynamics that the proposed structure would generate – and these dynamics are dealt with in greater detail in chapter 13.

12 The matter of taxation

Introduction
This chapter briefly explores the issue of taxation. It is relevant to the proposed new model of the corporation because this new model offers an opportunity to operate an entirely new approach to taxation that would have the effect of improving the prospects of employment even further and would articulate cohesively with our whole new philosophical approach to economic activity. It must be said, however, that the tax reform proposed could only be a practicality if the new corporate model were widely adopted as opposed to simply being one of a variety of trading frameworks available.

Government and taxation
Not all of society's needs are effectively provided by the market. Some things simply have to be provided nationally, or regionally, because otherwise they would never happen, or perhaps they would only happen haphazardly. This is in fact not just a *feature* of society, but one of the defining characteristics of civilisation itself: the act of collecting everyone together to organise those matters for which everyone's involvement or agreement is needed, or helpful. A civilised society *needs* a government, and, of course, a government needs to be funded. To put it succinctly, 'there is no market without government and no government without taxes' (Murphy & Nagel: 32).

Some of society's needs are therefore met by local, regional or national government: matters like defence, the legal system, the fire service, road and rail infrastructure, education, and the welfare of the needy, the sick and the least advantaged. Whether or not some of these can be organised, in part, along the lines of the market economy, nevertheless society's involvement as a whole is required.

It is very relevant that not everyone feels that they enjoy all the benefits provided by such expenditure; that not everyone is capable of contributing to its cost; and, ironically, that those who enjoy most of the benefits, often tend to be those who are least able to contribute to them at the time. That is precisely why the system is there. It is not unlike the concept of insurance. The extent of provision of all these services is a matter of politics and, in some measure, an indicator of civilised values.

Having said all this, it will be realised that government and business and human beings do not live in separate boxes, it all goes on at the same time and in the same place. All the systems therefore need to *integrate* comfortably, so that there is no unnecessary friction between the brutal disciplines of the market and the civilised benevolence of the State – nor, conversely, between the creative achievements of the market and the rigid, stifling regulation of the State. In other words, it makes sense for the interface between government, economic activity and society to be so arranged that State involvement is a natural and intrinsic part of the entirety of social activity. That is why a brief examination of taxation is included in this book.

In practical terms, therefore, if the cost of government can be integrated within the market economy, then we shall have the best of both worlds, civilised standards *and* the natural balance that the market provides. Two ways in which this might happen are explored in this book, one (a special tax on the corporation) for which the new corporate model is ideal and the other (environmental pricing: a subject on which many other writers have done much more work than this author) which matches the concept of the model but is unconnected with it.

Firstly, let's take a step back and look at our world today. How splendid, you may say, that fewer and fewer of us are now needed to spend all our time and effort producing the goods and services that we need for the survival, comfort and well-being of us all. Market economics, in conjunction with scientific and technological advance, has certainly driven the developed world closer than ever before to this natural and worthy goal. As a result, life is now so much richer and more comfortable for humankind in the western world.

It hasn't actually worked out quite so well, thanks to the inequalities of capitalism. But there is a further problem, too: that ever greater numbers are now dependent on a shrinking working population to sustain them. Yet if you read the previous paragraph again, surely that is precisely what we have been seeking to achieve by technological progress? If not, how else did we think that the result would appear? By needing fewer people to actually produce essential goods and services, there will by definition be more people idly consuming them.

The problem arises because we have an obsession, rooted in the historic past, that the source of funding for communal projects and for the least advantaged is the working individual. More specifically, we take from some individuals to give to others. This is an outdated idea, and we need to move away from the concept of taxing individual income and instead take *wealth creation* as the tax base. As GDP rises, it is only right in a civilised society for a rising amount of it to be set aside for the disadvantaged and the needy; after all, is that not what we mean by civilised values? There certainly *is* a problem for public expenditure today and for the future, but it is not the one of a reduced active workforce. Rather it is that we need to ensure that the burden of government expenditure is not increasing at such a rate that the actual amount of net wealth created by the community is insufficient to support it.

The proposed new corporate model offers us an opportunity to incorporate taxation within economic activity without distorting market pressures and in particular without increasing the cost of the labour contribution to economic activity.

Firstly, though, we need to briefly review the present operation of income tax.

Payroll taxes

During the tax year 2012/13, out of the total cost of central government, to the extent that it is raised through taxation, 46% was raised through income tax and national insurance (both of which are payroll taxes) and 54% through value added tax, corporation tax and other taxes.

The comparative figures for previous years were very similar; for 1988/89, for example, they were 44% and 56%. [*Source:* Office for Budget Responsibility, *Economic and Fiscal Outlook,* March 2012.]

In other words, nearly half of all tax revenue in the UK is raised 'through the payroll'. This does of course include tax raised by assessment, which is necessary for the self-employed taxpayers (who don't have a wage packet but pay taxes half-yearly on their calculated income) and in some other cases; it also includes tax on unearned income such as rent, dividends and interest. The point is, though, that nearly half of all tax revenue is taken from individuals *after* the market has fixed the appropriate level of their income.

Taxes in the UK are levied according to well-established principles that were laid down long ago by the great economist Adam Smith (Smith 1776): certainty, convenience, efficiency of collection, and burden proportionate to the ability to pay. Let us focus on this last principle. It obviously applies to all taxes, but is considered here in the context of income tax, and was eminently sensible at a time when there were few corporations, little economic activity as we know it today, and little 'economic wealth' such that the cost of government had to be borne in some way by asking those individual citizens who had the resources, to stump up their share of the burden.

But is such income tax still appropriate today, where it impacts on the vast majority of the working population, even on those in receipt of benefits, with almost half of routine public expenditure being paid for in this way?

If the operation of government is to be seen in the context of the market, then what government does is to provide the setting within which business activity can take place. So government is, in effect, an active shareholder or partner in each business. When a commercial entity receives income from its sales, some of that goes to pay other companies, some of it goes to the labour force, and some of it should go to pay the government for its contribution. A sharing of the fruits of economic activity at the point of its generation makes sense in the world of market economics: if economic activity (i.e., business) is the source of generation of private wealth, why should it not also be the source of generation of public wealth?

This book argues that the cost of government is not an individual responsibility, but a collective social one. It is argued that, in principle, taxation should not be levied on *exchanges* (i.e., individual income from economic activity) but on the *creation* of wealth (i.e., economic activity itself, which is the source of all income). It is otherwise like going round the family dinner table and removing food from each diner's plate to make up a plate for the grandparents: better to plate up each person's share from the same serving dishes in the kitchen.

Under our proposed new corporate model, the more wealth a business generates, the more the added value it can share among its participators, and government (both for its own purposes and for those it represents) should be one of those participators. It is the generation of economic activity by business and corporate enterprise that sustains the nation's population. Nothing else gets anywhere near it. It does this by paying wages, salaries, rents, interest, dividends, whatever. And in paying these amounts, it funds the payment of taxation out of them, so it is the perfect source for raising public revenue as well.

So, what exactly can we say is wrong with income tax? With income tax we must include what is called 'national insurance'. This is in fact no longer a form of insurance and is simply another payroll tax just like income tax. These two payroll taxes raise almost half the government's tax revenue, as indicated above. Our specific arguments against payroll taxes are set out below.

Firstly, income tax is a *depressing* tax. One philosopher, Robert Nozick, famously likened it to forced labour, and it is widely accepted by economists that payroll taxes distort the market for labour. They depress incentives to work harder, because they reduce the marginal benefit of doing so; and they depress employment because they raise the marginal cost of labour. They raise the price paid for a commodity (labour) higher than its value to the seller (the employee). The market economy's crucial foundation is division of labour: different people doing different things but swapping their value so that we each get what we want. Employment is the ultimate and most popular form of division of labour. Therefore to impose taxes, which increase the labour cost without benefiting the employee, is positively harmful in a market economy.

Secondly, there is universal resentment about paying a tax on income, because it is a distortion of the price allocation processes. It charges a burden on individuals *after* their proper share of what their contribution is worth has already been allocated to them by the market. Individuals see the tax as being a mandatory removal by the State of their own money for purposes over which they have no personal control. The fact that this isn't actually the case makes no difference: in reality the money that the tax represents was never theirs in the first place. The individual would never have received his wage without the efforts of the business he works for, and that business would not have happened without the government structure being there. The tax therefore is really no more than the cost of any other supplier to the business, and so ought to be borne directly at the source of economic wealth, which is the company as employer. Then the share of that wealth as allocated *by the market* to each employee would be precisely what that employee is worth, and this would be precisely what he receives.

Thirdly, the abolition of income tax would not only reduce the huge costs of collection, it would also nicely eliminate a major part of the 'black economy'. This would make tax more efficient, as the overall rate payable would be lower if fewer people evaded it. It would also reduce the distortion in the reported figures, and therefore make macro-economic management more efficient.

Fourthly and finally, if we did away with payroll taxes, there would be a major shift in the definition of economic viability as far as employees are concerned. Not only would more marginal staff be employed, but more marginal businesses (especially those in labour-intensive industries) would survive, because their total employment costs would fall, thus protecting the employment of existing staff. Admittedly, the most marginal staff would have little liability to payroll tax, but overall, the cost of employing people would fall in comparison with other costs.

Let us return to the first criticism outlined above. Payroll taxes are so called because the amount of such tax paid is related directly to the amount of gross wages paid (the 'payroll') and the tax liability is incurred at the same time as the wages are paid. It may not be appreciated by some readers just how much of a burden payroll taxes are in their obstruction of market forces. For a person on average earnings in 2014-15, each £100 of additional take-home pay for the employee involves the employer paying a total cost of £167.35, plus he may need to charge VAT on top of this. Imagine a gardening company with a customer who has a job to be done worth £100. That is the market value of the job, and what the customer is prepared to pay. After taking off VAT, and accounting for tax and national insurance, the employee has to be prepared to do that job for £49.80. No wonder there is a black economy in such jobs! The work has to be worth £100 to the householder, yet less than £50 to the person doing it – and that leaves no margin whatever to cover advertising, insurance, tools and equipment, or health and safety and other employment regulation costs, let alone any profit for the gardening company.

If it only cost the gardening company employer £50 to put £50 of net wages into the hands of the employee: then he'd employ twice as many people! There would be an explosion in employment, and many of those initially marginal staff would hopefully end up as core employees under the proposed new company structure. There must be a better way to raise taxation than to punish employment.

Further problems with income tax

One of the perceived merits of an income tax is that it is 'progressive': richer people (or rather those on higher incomes) pay more than poorer people, thereby achieving some automatic redistribution of wealth. But does it actually achieve this? Those on higher incomes tend to have good accountants and so pay less tax than those without. If not, then they demand tax-free benefits or even higher pay rises to cover the extra tax due; and generally, they are in the position to demand this, so the cost of their taxation is effectively paid by everyone else (as it comes out of the total economic wealth created).

Another perceived merit of income tax is that it can be tampered with to give various tax allowances to seemingly deserving causes. A person providing for her future through pension contributions pays less tax than one saving for her retirement by investing in property. A one-man-band business investing in lots of brand new equipment is likely to pay proportionately less tax than a hard-up individual who has to rent some machinery, or make do with second-hand equipment. But are such tax breaks really justified? Do they actually *work* in terms of influencing decision-making in the 'right' way? If such incentives really are necessary (and many commentators seriously doubt this) then why not have the government pay a transparently clear subsidy directly to those causes that are deemed to be politically right to encourage?

Income tax, when levied on investment income (i.e., on income from savings), does discourage investment and favour consumption, which is unhelpful to long-term economic growth. Why should accumulated income, which has already suffered tax when it was earned, be taxed again just because it was not frittered away? Most forms of personal savings find their way eventually into corporate investment and therefore into productive capital. Taxing investment income is often seen as a sneaky way of taxing capital: if this is a good thing, then why not tackle the issue head-on and ensure that capital does not receive more than it's really worth, as in our proposed new corporate model?

But all of these criticisms of income tax are already accepted by most economic commentators. What they don't agree on is the solution, and here the new model of the corporation could well be the answer. That is why the issue of taxation appears in this book.

It must be acknowledged that there is one area in which income tax can be justified. Some extremely large incomes – those of internationally celebrated entertainers, writers, sportsmen, artists and so on – have a feature that differentiates them from others. A case can be made that the size of their income is only in one part due to special talent, and in another part due directly to the sheer size of the consumer market available to them. The community has, through technology and globalisation, magnified that person's audience and therefore his income. To the extent that a person enjoys increased income *thanks to* the size of the consumer base, that person might be regarded as having a *quasi-debt due* to consumers. This debt could then be discharged by contributing redistributive taxes to that society. To put this another way, individual effort is a private contribution worthy of private reward, but the benefits of globalisation are more of a communal asset, for which the community needs to see some reward through taxation. This would justify income tax being levied on some of the highest incomes only.

An equity profits tax?

If it is accepted that government is necessary, then it does need to be paid for. It is difficult to conceive how it can be paid for, other than by means of what we conveniently call taxes. Later in this chapter, we make out the case for a tax based on environmental pricing, but to the extent that this raises insufficient revenue, how should the shortfall best be raised? Over the past half century, industrial countries have gradually shifted towards *indirect* taxes on consumption (VAT, sales tax, etc.) rather than direct taxes on income, possibly for some of the reasons outlined above. But indirect taxes can be very regressive, and it seems wrong that the very poorest have to contribute along with everyone else.

Is there some other means of raising tax that does not interfere with the best operational principles of the free market? Yes, there is. Earlier in this chapter, we explained how the government might effectively be viewed as a participator in business enterprise. The government's share of the profit would be no different from anyone else's. Under the proposed system of 'equity units', an appropriate proportion of the value added by each corporation would be the appropriate tax liability. Simple to calculate, cheap and straightforward to collect. Being based on value added, it would not distort in any way the structure of supply and demand, or the mechanics of viability. It would be different from corporation tax in that it would be charged on the 'profit' *before* sharing out any equity profits, whether payable to employees or anyone else, i.e., it would be based precisely on the value added to society by the corporation.

Such a value-added tax would have some of the merits of the existing VAT, but would avoid one substantial disadvantage: it would not be based on identifying value added by reference to individual sales and purchases invoices. Why is this done with VAT? This is partly because the present system, which in the UK developed out of 'purchase tax' which was invoice-based, is preferred by HM Revenue & Customs on the grounds that it makes the amount due doubly verifiable. The purchase invoices of one business are of course the sales invoices of another business. It also lends itself to relatively easy self-assessment on a quarterly or monthly basis.

This unfortunate obsession with mechanics destroys the conceptual validity of value added as put forward in this book and reduces VAT to little more than a selective retail sales tax. By utilising a system of 'inputs' and 'outputs', it also involves a huge accounting operation and masses of complex regulations in order to achieve what could be much more simple. Most businesses think in 'net of VAT' terms with regard to prices (all business price lists, for example, routinely exclude VAT) and therefore VAT is simply added to the price. If the VAT rate rises, the price goes up. As a result, the tax becomes little different from a sales tax upon consumers, and therefore directly influences consumer decisions.

In many cases this can lead to absurd results, where different rates of VAT apply to different types of sales. A typical example in recent years was that of the baker: if he sells his sausage rolls nice and warm because they have just come out of the oven, then he is charged no VAT, but if he then puts some of them in a heated cabinet for two minutes to keep them warm, he *is* charged VAT at the full rate; he has to have different means to account for the different sales quite separately – any mistakes (even innocent ones) can lead to substantial penalties. If you buy a derelict cottage (so derelict that just the four walls remain) and totally renovate it for your own occupation, you cannot claim any of the VAT back, as this is a repair. This will set you back thousands of pounds. But if you bulldoze the four walls and build them up again from the foundations, then you can reclaim all the VAT you suffer because you are building a new property.

A further problem with VAT is that there has to be a level of trading below which you do not need to 'join the club'. As a result, traders who are not quite small enough, perhaps because they are trying to do things professionally, are (with VAT at 20%) a full 20% more expensive to consumers than those not joining the club. This severely discourages the very small businesses that serve the general public from growing into more worthwhile enterprises. Compulsory registration at the threshold (currently £81,000 for 2014-15) can cost a labour-intensive business, such as a self-employed plumber or carpenter with few VAT-able expenses but one or two employees, as much as £16,000 (at 20% VAT) – as much as a fulltime employee on the minimum wage – and cut the net profit down to less than the employee gets.

Finally, any tax which simply increases retail prices evenly across the board is 'regressive', i.e., it bites harder into the resources of poorer people than richer people (as basic living costs tend to be fixed). It therefore not only disturbs market forces, but does so in a particularly harmful way. For this reason, it is helpful to have a tax that does *not* tend to increase a retail price above whatever figure market demand has set. Therefore there is considerable merit in a *value added tax* being based not on sales invoices but on *total value added* by a business enterprise in a particular period, such as a year. Interim payments can still be made if necessary for cash flow purposes, but there is no sound reason why the annual calculation of value added for tax purposes cannot be precisely the same as for the equity holders' own purposes. The 'equity profits tax' is then truly borne at the source of generation of economic wealth, i.e., where value is added.

Tax avoidance
Are there any particular avoidance risks to be considered?

Every business with any sort of dealings with the public would need to be registered in some way. This would ensure that it was 'caught' for tax, as well as giving the database for health and safety enforcement and for some level of public trading standards protection. Instead of having a 'Companies Registry' recording a lot of detail on companies and nothing at all on other businesses, it is difficult to argue against a 'Business Registry' that would record for public inspection the essential information about every registered business. At present, every single business has to register anyway, but this is with the HM Revenue & Customs, where the information provided is then held confidentially. At the lowest level, an individual would need to decide whether to be a 'casual' employee of another business or to be a registered business on his own account (or both). It is to be hoped that registration would not be difficult or costly as it would need to be encouraged; it would also need to be immediately apparent – a registered number would have to be clearly shown. To some extent there would be market pressure as non-registered businesses would have no health and safety cover, no insurances, and no come-back in the event of faulty work or faulty goods. If the protection for the customer were sufficient, and the cost and effort to the business fairly minimal, registration would be widespread.

What would happen about the very smallest businesses? For example, domestic employees or window cleaners? An individual purely selling his own labour isn't adding value to the market, he's making a living. There is an element of absurdity in the concept of economic activity at this level: imagine two neighbours who each look after the other's children and tend the other's garden, charging appropriately equal sums to each other. In that street there would be much economic activity (contributing to Britain's GDP) yet, if instead they were to only look after their own children and do their own gardening (a change having no real impact on society), there would be none.

Minor self-employment would not generate taxation. But as soon as someone employs any core staff or has partners, or engages other 'equity contributors' then they become an economic entity and the taxation requirement would follow.

It will be obvious that one major source of avoidance (and indeed evasion) will be eliminated, and that is the problem of individuals under-declaring their income. If income tax as we know it is withdrawn, then the problem of individuals suppressing their income will disappear completely.

Would there be any other avoidance risks?

Businesses might pay their core staff much higher wages (instead of providing equity units to them) so as to reduce the equity profits. To some extent, this would be a free market decision and is even something to be applauded, but there will be a limit to the extent to which the unit holders would want to reduce the profits for their own purposes, as that is precisely the same figure that the tax is paid on. Few businesses today are likely to pay higher wages to staff in order to reduce their corporation tax.

Potential criticisms

Firstly, such a proposal would clearly not be a practical proposition unless the proposed new corporate model was the standard model for corporate enterprise in the UK. This is something to work towards, but would not happen overnight.

Secondly, you may ask how the proposed taxation of equity units would differ from existing corporation tax, which most economists say is better when the tax rate is lower?

Corporation tax is charged on corporate profits before dividends are paid, so it could be argued that a corporation tax rate of 20%, for example, is no different to the government owning a fifth of equity units, so that the other equity holders can then only enjoy what's left. In that sense there is little difference. There would of course be certain international implications, which are dealt with elsewhere. Yet many commentators would argue that a higher corporation tax rate for the UK would be bad for the UK economy, and of course a higher rate (or more accurately, a greater sum per company) would be necessary to compensate for the absence of income tax and national insurance. A high corporation tax rate is said to discourage companies from setting up in this country; it would encourage companies to have their head office (and consequently pay tax) elsewhere, yet still trade within the UK.

Our response is that the total corporate outgoings in respect of taxation (i.e., combining what's now paid in payroll taxes with existing corporation tax) would be precisely the same as it is at present: all that would be different is that labour costs would be precisely what the market sets (i.e., lower), and the cost of taxation would be seen to be what it truly was. The taxation cost in fact might well be slightly lower as the cost of collection would be rather lower. Moreover, with wage costs much lower (benefiting from what would be equivalent to a massive subsidy), there should be more employment and so more value added to the market, and thus the tax cost as such should again be a smaller proportion of corporate surpluses.

The problem is in fact not *real* but *comparative*. If all companies worked along the lines of the new model, there would be no problem at all. The threat, insofar as there is one, comes from low-tax foreign jurisdictions. With present international pressure to harmonise corporation tax rates, or at least to reduce blatant evasion, this issue in itself may start to fade. In any event, the political pressure to reduce corporate tax rates will continue: there will be no change there.

A further potential criticism is that the payroll taxes presently raised from employees of non-corporate tax paying employers would need to be raised by some other means, because there will be no equity profits tax here to compensate for it. The answer is that such employers are likely to be in the public service sector, i.e., local or national government employees of one type or another, and of course the payroll taxes that will be missed won't any longer have to be raised and paid for by corporate taxes elsewhere. In other words, public employees won't contribute payroll taxes, but corporate taxes won't have to be raised to pay for that portion of the cost either: the total taxation requirement will be that much less.

The only area where there will be some unavoidable impact is in relation to charities and similar not-for-profit organisations. However, if the work done by these bodies qualifies in some way as a 'charitable public service', which is what one presumes, then there can hardly be criticism if the tax system provides them with some advantage. In any event, in the context of the national economy, the amount involved is unlikely to be material.

The environment

In tracing the history of the present form of corporation, we have seen earlier in this book how economics as a science has trailed behind the history of man rather than helping to shape it. When the foundations of modern economics were being laid, our predecessors took the world as it was then, for good or bad, rather than imagining how it might become. The wealthy European man saw himself as master of the Earth: the very planet had in his view been made for nothing other than his own pleasure, and economics was the science needed to help him make the most of this. Natural produce was simply plucked from the trees, or gathered up from the ground; energy was barely thought of except in the Doldrums; labour was abundant and extremely servile; even enterprise was everywhere. All that was in short supply was the one ingredient that seemed to make business happen, namely wealth – and this was concentrated in the hands of a tiny minority with no 'market' to make it accessible.

Thus it was understandable that economists at the time should have identified possessors of *capital* as being the absolute owner not only of all commerce but also of natural resources, with 'rent' being due to the freehold owner for the use of this. Three separate propositions can be identified from this, and each one needs to be challenged as flawed in today's world:

1. With a hugely increased population devouring them, we now realise that natural resources are not unlimited. We are aware that there are real limitations in the availability of all natural resources and products, whether this is timber, minerals, energy, wildlife, mountains, beaches, clean air, food, living space, land, even fish in the sea. As yet, it is simply not a practical proposition to think in terms of humans colonising other planets (whether or not that is a suitable or proper thing to do one day) and therefore we have to accept that all the world's resources are both *scarce* and *valuable* to us. We are in danger of reaching the limits of sustainability in many areas.

2. We have a human population, every single one of whom we now recognise as having a legitimate aspiration to participate in the functioning of society. Not only that, but they *need* to participate if we are to avoid a serious disturbance of social harmony. What this means is that the need to involve people is becoming recognised as more important than the traditional desire to simply use them for the benefit of the owners of commerce. Thus *involving* people is starting to become a goal in itself rather than being a cost to be minimised.

3. With greater breadth of access to capital, and the greater flow of capital patiently queuing up to be invested – banks and building societies advertising their keenness to lend, monthly pension contributions and life assurance premiums flooding in – capital

for business, while still being an undeniably scarce resource, is being accepted now as only *one* of the inputs necessary for the organisation of business enterprise.

The second and third propositions have already been covered earlier in this book as they are central to the new model of the corporation. But just as our proposals argue that there should be no *absolute* permanent ownership of a corporation, we now similarly argue that some things belong *to the community* rather than to the individual. In the closing part of this chapter we shall therefore now look more closely at the first of these propositions, which is now becoming much more widely accepted (indeed, this is an area in which others have done much more work than this author), and, while it is not directly required for the proposed new corporate model, it certainly integrates with it.

Value and price
It is a fundamental concept of market economics that, if something is valuable but of limited availability, then it has a price, and the greater its value or limited availability, then the greater that price is likely to be. If the great classical economists had lived today, they would most certainly have concluded (as do many modern commentators) that all natural products and resources should carry a price, and that this price should be the full 'market' price. As it is, no cost is at present attributed to the consumption of limited natural resources, or to pollution or damage to natural amenities, or to anything else which gradually exhausts the limited supply. Thus the proper economic and social cost of resource exploitation, wastage and violation of the environment is not taken into account in economic decision-making, except perhaps as a superficial public relations exercise, and as a result, there are no *direct* market pressures brought to bear to exercise restraint or moderation.

Imagine if we could establish a system of allocation of market prices on sustainability: this would bring its true cost into the mechanics of everyday economic decision-making and therefore *influence* those decisions in a natural and automatic way. Not only that, but there would be a further bonus: the system would actually raise revenue for the government, it would yield taxation which could be applied to reduce taxes in other areas, such as income tax.

Despite its free market credentials, the typical western government is still one of the largest and most dominant offenders to the market economy. Its cost, through taxation, is unilaterally imposed and arbitrarily allocated by *diktat*. It makes no effort to work with the grain of legitimate market forces; its effect on the market is justified as correcting some of the intrinsic inequities of the market (for example, in its redistributive effect), but it is plainly susceptible to pure political expediency, rather than being an attempt at a comprehensive assessment of the proper reaction to current market failings. As explained in the previous chapter, much taxation deeply disfavours the very idea of employment, perversely taxing the creation of employment, and actively discouraging the participation of human beings in business – thereby creating for employers (even the one-man business employing a single assistant) a huge minefield of aggressive legislation with extensive, rigid financial penalties.

By contrast, a simple but systematic policy of commercially pricing all limited resources would have dramatic consequences: the putting of an economic value on what we all most treasure, tangible pressure to cut down on waste and pollution, an *economic* encouragement to recycle and sustain. There would be a *reason* for tackling the routine exhaustion of nature, and there would be a reduction in unemployment, by relief from payroll taxes.

Environmental pricing has certainly become a much more accepted idea today, and there is already an extensive literature on it, but because it fits in so well with the proposed changes to the corporate model, a brief outline of it is included in this book.

The main problem, of course, is that for environmental pricing to be done properly, it needs to be introduced on a global scale. Some efforts towards this have been introduced in limited areas, such as carbon pricing and even in the use of disposable plastic bags, but these small efforts are often little more than gestures. Once we accept the principle, however, we are then left with the problem of the mechanics. Moreover, there are problems to be addressed such as its inflationary pressure, the matter of export pricing, and the impact on resource-rich countries.

This chapter is obviously far too short to provide a full analysis of the issue, but it can provide the pointers. There is plenty of other literature available on many of the ideas that are touched on here.

Conclusion

What is likely to be the effect of environmental pricing as a full or partial replacement for payroll taxes?

1. By more nearly equating the cost of wages to their value to the recipient, the friction that hinders employment is reduced. Labour, quite simply, becomes cheaper to employ. This should help to reduce unemployment.

2. Environmental damage, pollution and wastage of natural resources should reduce as there would be a cost punishment for this: the polluter pays.

3. There would be a positive economic reason to seek sustainability, to encourage recycling and to pursue healthier, possibly organic methods in agriculture.

4. There would be a cultural shift away from the disposable society and a greater concentration on maintaining rather than replacing, on quality of manufacture, on getting things right first time.

5. The environment would be a healthier place for human beings.

6. The previously irreconcilable conflict between the demands of economic growth and its effect on the natural world should start to be resolved.

The classical economists did actually recognise that natural resources were in limited supply, but their response was to attribute the right of 'economic rent' to the owner of the resource. This therefore supposed that the resource was actually *provided* by whichever individual person happened to have the legal title to it and, by attributing the rent to the owner, it made an already arbitrary misallocation of wealth even worse. Today it is more readily accepted that the community as a whole has the ownership of and responsibility for natural resources.

Obviously this analysis brings to light the unworkability of the traditional and now rather dated concept of permanent and absolute private ownership, where this is more than just an occupational right. But things are moving that way already, and the tide is likely to gather pace. The traditional concept of ownership of the corporate framework has already been challenged in this book – by reducing equity ownership to the rights of those currently contributing to its success – and here is its logical extension in the wider context. It provides a reality to the notion of stewardship; it calls for justification how any section of mankind has the simple authority to confer absolute title to property, when it is now being realised that all of us have a legitimate interest in the careful husbandry of so much of it.

13 Summary of the proposals for a new corporate model

The trouble with capitalism: some of the detailed failings of the present limited company corporate model

1   The out-dated assumption that capital is the sole driving force behind enterprise, so the return on capital has to be maximised while other contributions are minimised. This makes the model inflexible and artificial: it doesn't match reality. It is lop-sided, being driven awkwardly from one edge of the 'circle of participators' instead of from the heart of enterprise. As a result, all participators in economic activity *other* than capital providers are treated as economic servants, so that their reward from that activity is pruned to the minimum for the sole benefit of the capital provider.

2   The model requires that shareholders will act as the supervisors of the directors, yet they are quite simply the wrong people for that task. Their interest (in public companies) is usually limited to buy/sell/hold decisions on their shares; if they are not entirely happy with things, they can simply 'cop out' and sell their shares. They are not, in general, sufficiently interested or involved enough in the undertaking to want to help monitor it properly.

3   For those shareholders who are interested in becoming more involved in their company, the possibilities (particularly in public companies) are bleak. Their practical experience of participation in the creation, control and supervision of industry

and commerce is limited to their meeting each other and the directors once a year for a couple of hours in a formal, soulless and often confrontational setting; the shareholders receive a single report once a year, written by the directors upon themselves; they are not an organised group and, once they have invested their money, they have no further executive function other than to passively ratify proposals put to them by the board of directors. It would not be entirely unfair to compare their position in practice with that of the electorate in a one-party state.

4   The contestability of corporate bosses by hostile take-over rather than by proper challenge by the company's own shareholders at their AGM is hailed by some commentators as the preferred weapon of supervision: hardly different from the contestability of dictators by a military coup. Is that to be the proud end product of all the corporate governance and stewardship regulation in the UK?

5   The feeble position of the minority shareholder in a private limited company: if she owns less than one half of the company, and is not also a director, then as private companies rarely pay dividends (the directors as the largest shareholders often pay themselves substantial bonuses as directors and have unfettered power to do so) and there is no market for resale of the shares, she can become completely isolated and see her shares become virtually worthless.

6   The unsatisfactory position of employees for whose significant contribution there is little statutory recognition, other than outside the Companies Acts. There is a need for the input of the workforce, the individuals who actually do all the work that makes the corporation what it is, to be recognised *structurally* in the framework of the corporation. Their voice needs to be heard, and they also need to have some share in the rewards from their contribution to economic activity, but this needs to be done in a businesslike way.

7   The lack of relevance that equity shares have, in an established company, to true participation in commercial or industrial

activity. It could be argued that investing in the Stock Exchange by buying existing shares has now become so far removed from the reality of actually funding industrial enterprise that it is almost comparable to pure gambling on the form and performance of racehorses. As noted above, most shareholders regard their shareholding as a means to make a few pounds of easy capital gain, and simply fail to acknowledge that they have any responsibility for exercising control or supervision over the directors.

8   The high degree of exposure to loss frequently required of unsecured trading suppliers, without any structural recognition of the value of their contribution or of their need to be informed of the extent of their risk.

9   The effective domination by the directors, who need have no qualifications, experience or capital risk, is not adequately recognised statutorily, with little formal control or monitoring, no built-in sanctions for their failures and no statutory formula for the bargaining of their reward. They are expected to set their own salaries and bonuses, with not even a specific system in place to require formal shareholder approval for this. The directors are not generally personally responsible for the outcome of their decisions in any way, and there is far more supervision or monitoring of their affairs by bankers (who are secured) than by shareholders (who in theory are completely at risk).

10 The vulnerability of publicly-quoted companies to hostile take-overs on the basis that the share capital gives the right to all that a business is and does, and all that it owns, right down to the furthest subsidiary, without the slightest reference to the workforce or others deeply committed to or involved in the company. The power this confers is reminiscent of the control an empire used to have over its colonial dominions, with the benefits of colonial natural resources being forcibly possessed by the distant owner. Major football clubs for example can be owned and controlled as playthings by total strangers who have no connection with the team and no contact with fans. The imposition of an external objective or 'mission', different from

that of the target company and often incompatible with its existing participators, can destroy the essence and integrity of that business to the detriment of all those involved in it. The traditional corporation can be little more than a mere chattel for those with capital, while others who give their lifetimes to it have no standing at all.

11 The mission of an enterprise being in practice generally decided by one or two of the most dominating individuals among the directors with little or no reference to shareholders or other participators. Even the constitution (the Memorandum and Articles of Association) now recognises this in the collapse of the concept of the Objects Clause.

12 The fact that it is the directors who prepare the annual report and accounts which are then passively audited and presented to the shareholders, with a copy eventually filed for public inspection. The annual accounts themselves are more of a historical record than anything else. Rarely does anyone in command of a business actually rely solely on such accounts for decision-making, so it is contemptuous to expect the ultimate owner or any other participator to do so. The annual accounts are mechanically structured and stereotyped, having to conform strictly to the format specified in the Companies Acts: such comparability with other companies being in the interest of and for the benefit of shareholders who trade in the shares rather than being long-term investors.

13 The ineffective position of the auditors, who are in practice selected, appointed and paid by the directors. They work with them and (in effect) report to them, having no direct contact with the shareholders as such. The findings expressed in their report tend to be set out in a formulaic and 'boilerplate' fashion, with standardised wording. They do not give their own frank, fearless and objective report on what they themselves find in the company, but are only required to give limited assurances that the directors' account and presentation complies with the rules, i.e., is not actually untruthful and not actually unfair.

14   The fact that the auditors have a statutory duty only to the share capital providers, and have no specific responsibility whatever to creditors, employees or any other person with a material stake in the company, despite the fact that these persons are known to rely heavily on the published, audited accounts.

15   The failure in many cases of non-executive directors to be the independent authority as envisaged in the 'Cadbury Code', instead of simply assisting the main directors. They suffer from an inherent conflict of interest as both a director and a supervisor of directors at the same time; they are selected by, appointed by, paid by and, in practical terms, answerable to the directors they are supposed to supervise; and they have no independent legitimate authority or power base to support them.

16   The complete sham of the £2 limited company which is little more than a sole trader, bought off the shelf for £100, dilatory in filing, with the director treating the company's cash as if it were his own, and often quite disinterested that innocent and unsuspecting creditors might lose out completely.

17   The absurdity of having all corporate economic activity measured in terms of a return on capital rather than on value added to the market. This does not maximise economic growth; it discourages marginal yet profitable business ventures; it acts to minimise and therefore depress employment; it promotes ever-increasing inequality by depressing wage costs and rewarding capital providers.

18   The extreme rigidity of the model, which is only capable of recognising share capital providers as valuable participants, who are then structurally rewarded for evermore. There is no recognition of other participants, and no flexibility to reflect changes in circumstances. Other potential contributors to the corporation have to devise schemes to pretend that they are new, additional shareholders in order to share in the equity profits and the equity control.

19   One of the objections to directors or employees being rewarded by having share incentives is that, not only is it an artificial

device (i.e., a pretence that they are also shareholders), but it also provides the *wrong* incentive. It motivates them to do whatever is necessary to raise the share price for the period for which it applies. Not only does this encourage short-term policies, but more importantly, it leads to excessive pressure on wages and suppliers and others in order to transfer the financial advantage to shareholders. This latter activity is not in the interests of the corporation itself, nor of customers or the community as a whole, as it aims to benefit one participator to the detriment of everyone else.

20 The extreme distancing of actual ownership from meaningful participation creates a dichotomy between 'them' and 'us': 'them' that own the company, yet have remarkably little involvement in it or attachment to it, and 'us' that actually identify our lives with the company, produce the profits and yet have little statutory recognition or reward. This could be said to have led to the abasement of the whole culture of corporate economic activity, such that the very word 'corporate' (as in the corporate class of air traveller, the corporate hotel bedroom, and even the 'corporate day out') has now become synonymous with the sense of "don't worry, it's not my money". It is as rare for a director (other than one who is also a major shareholder) to treat his company's money as if it were his own, as it is for an employee to choose and operate a company car as he would his own.

21 The existing corporate model generates inequality by cornering the benefits of the economic activity of all the other participators, and then handing those rewards solely to the shareholder. The major component of the inequality of wealth in the world is in the possession of corporate stocks, i.e., ownership of shares in companies, and the traditional 'capitalist' corporation relentlessly increases that inequality by having a framework that converts the efforts of everyone in business into a reward for the possessor of capital. Furthermore, success of corporate activity is measured in terms of value earned for the shareholders; often much of this is not actually the result of economic growth (the whole of that extra 'value' has not been

added to the market) but more the effect of reducing rewards for other participators and transferring these to the shareholders.

Summary of the proposals

The proposals put forward in this book in relation to the introduction of a new corporate model could be summarised briefly as follows:

1   The directors, and not the capital providers, are the driving force of enterprise, and should therefore be at the heart of the corporation.

2   Risk capital is just one of the participators in economic activity. Other participators (such as management, workforce or suppliers) can have as much, or even greater, value to the corporation, depending on the circumstances of each case, and the model provides for this in a structural way, while at the same time having the flexibility to cope with major changes as they happen. Nothing is fixed rigidly.

3   If the model is driven from its centre, i.e., by the directors, then it can be seen that the interests of the corporation are no longer synonymous with those of one class of participator, i.e., the shareholders. Instead, the directors can now act in the true best interests of the corporation as a whole (i.e., the whole body of participators) in striking the most appropriate balance between the rewards necessary for each contributory, depending of course on the inputs necessary. Precisely where this balance should be struck will vary from one corporation to another and, within any particular corporation, from one point in time to another. This is achieved by dissociating equity from share capital, and enabling 'equity units' to be isolated as a separate valuable commodity to be bargained for by any of the contributories (directors, capital, workforce, suppliers, etc.) in accordance with well-established free market principles.

4   The equity is in the hands of the directors and is parcelled out by them according to the established principles of the market economy bargaining mechanism, in order to create a workable team of equity holders. The directors deal as necessary with the

issuing, redeeming, cancelling and re-issuing of such equity units.

5   Because the equity unit holders have, by definition, real relevance to the conduct of the corporation's affairs, they will want to be more actively involved than is generally the case with shareholders. They are therefore likely to welcome the specific proposals made for a more cohesive and effective working relationship between themselves and the directors in order to maximise overall direction and control. This in turn requires a fresh conceptual approach to corporate governance.

6   The nature of 'share capital' is examined, and it is recognised that the risk profile changes with time and company performance. It follows that the reward necessary for share capital reduces once its vulnerability reduces, and this is the source of increasing reward then available to the other participators, in particular the management and workforce upon whose efforts the success of the corporation now largely depends.

7   Built into the system is an incentive to retain profits and increase reserves, because with a more powerfully independent corporation, fewer equity units need to be given away to outsiders to help with capital raising and sudden emergencies. Keeping the equity within the corporation means that those most intimately involved and strategically committed to it, which would normally be the directors and the workforce, are then effectively in charge of it and responsible for it – and receive the rewards.

8   The general concept of limited liability is reviewed, and seen to have a flawed theoretical basis from any perspective other than that of the traditional equity capital provider. Far from being a stimulant to business, it is argued to be a major cause of the failure of other well-run companies whose supplies, in good faith, have not been paid for.

9   The needs, and the concept, of financial reporting have undergone something of a revolution in the last seventy years,

while the concept of auditing remains rooted in the distant past. A radical and yet remarkably simple revision of the auditor's passive role is proposed, so as to make it more active and truly objective.

10 A corporation's net output would be directly identified with 'value added' for the market and society as a whole, rather than being a matter of the rate of net profit for capital providers, this change in the meaning of 'equity' bringing the ideal motivation to corporate activity. More goods and services would be produced, and the benefits shared out more equally among all those who have made the effort to produce them.

Introduction of the new model

There is no reason in principle why an existing private limited company – or even an unlimited company – cannot be converted into the new form of corporation. Clearly, a new constitution will be necessary, but this could be adopted with the agreement of all existing shareholders.

Similarly, there is no reason why the new form of corporation cannot co-exist alongside the present limited company, just as that co-exists with sole traders and partnerships.

Thinking it through...

What exactly would the *practical* effects be if the structure outlined above were introduced as the new corporate model? These have all been fully discussed in earlier parts of this book, but it may be helpful to collect them all together here.

1 The company would be under the control of those persons currently most critically contributing to it, as chosen according to established free market principles, and these same persons would automatically share all the profits and losses resulting. They would be the equity holders, and their best interests (and those of the directors who would be among their number) would be synonymous with the best interests of the corporation as a whole. This is wholly different from the present model, which literally exists for the sole benefit of the capital providers; as a result, everyone else who presently participates in the corporation (and this includes the workforce, the suppliers and

even the customers) is regarded as an economic servant to be exploited in order to maintain an externally-set share price. This has been the driving force of inequality, adding to the stock of wealth of those with capital and taking it from everyone else. The new model would lead to a reduction in inequality for all those involved in corporate activity: inequality in both the concept of participation and in the financial rewards resulting from it. Even customers would benefit.

2   The equity holders will have been specifically chosen by the directors for their contribution, instead of being a random collection of persons often far removed from the business itself, and rarely wanting to be involved. There will be a more meaningful regime of supervision by the equity holders, and their approach to corporate governance will be far more positive. Once the number of them exceeds, say, half a dozen, they could elect a committee of their number to act as 'governors', and this small committee might productively meet with the directors once a month or once a quarter for informal discussions on company progress.

Directors and employees presently resent the ownership by shareholders whose involvement and commitment appear to be so much less than theirs; shareholders for their part often resent their feeble and often rather meaningless involvement. With equity holders being more directly relevant and more involved, the corporation becomes more of a focused and self-organising entity. The committee of governors would be a more effective body to carry out the functions currently aspired to by non-executive directors (or even the chairman) in exerting more influence upon the board of directors and challenging instances of poor management. The governors would, after all, actually represent the owners of the company. They would be the natural body to select and appoint auditors, who might then be their expert arm to prepare their own independent report on the financial position of the company, actually preparing the accounts that bear their name.

3   Directors would be at the heart of things rather than the shareholders. The present form of company is owned by one of its participators, and this makes it awkwardly lop-sided. What

should happen is that the more successful a corporation becomes, the cheaper its cost of capital (the cost of servicing its risk capital) should be, thereby enabling a greater surplus to be available to be shared among all those producing it. Today, the opposite happens: the cost of capital rises as the company gets more successful. The share price goes up and so dividends have to rise – and to make that happen, all the other participators in economic activity (those actually producing the surplus) have to be squeezed more and more. This creates unfair inequality, and produces an illegitimate idea of economic growth. The old-fashioned model is a static linear concept, while the proposed new model is a dynamic concentric form, with the directors at the heart or centre of the company, and all the participators – the equity holders – are in a surrounding circle, constantly feeding back. Those capital providers seeking the highest returns – and richly deserving of them – would under the new model have to recycle their funds into new enterprises (offering a higher proportion of equity units) every five or ten years instead of leaving the capital to stagnate. This in turn should release more risk capital for new ventures. Low-risk permanent funding capital might attract a lower return: the actual rate is a matter for market forces to decide.

4   Successful directors would be remunerated in a structured way. Instead of having to contrive and defend selfish service contracts, share option schemes and fringe benefits, they could have a basic salary and then rely entirely and openly on long-term equity units for their real bonus. Their motivation will to that extent then be synonymous with the general body of equity holders, plus an incentive to go for long-term benefits that will secure a greater share of the equity for themselves. The beauty of market economics is that you can entirely do away with price justification and value judgement: by bringing the free market to the heart of the corporation, directors' rewards are set wholly by the laws of supply and demand.

5   The core workforce can at long last be structurally involved in the vital conceptual feature of participation, so that that ancient remnant of the feudal system, the master/servant relationship, may finally be disposed of. Equity rewards given to core

employees become an appropriation of profit rather than an expense, so that the provision of employment is a successful achievement, not a control failure.

6   The workforce and the management will both be structurally involved in the ownership and direction of established businesses. The equity holders and directors will be more directly and frequently involved with each other. Equity holders will be only those participating actively in the corporation. For these three reasons, there is likely to be greater cohesion between management and workforce in established corporations: they will have a common purpose, and be on the same side.

7   The proposed model creates an opportunity to allow a completely fresh threshold of 'economic viability' to be available for commercial decision-making, both for the corporation as a whole and for individual projects within it. The new model permits the viability of an enterprise so long as there is any positive value-added at all, sufficient to reward those prepared to carry out the work concerned. Having to achieve a minimum level of 'return on capital' so as to maintain the share price would cease. This should dramatically increase the potential for those marginal businesses that would otherwise close down – and thereby reduce unnecessary unemployment. The same effect would apply to individual projects, which would not necessarily be rejected simply because their profitability was insufficient to maintain the level of return on capital required by a specific share price.

8   There is greater capacity to temporarily reduce total labour costs without necessarily cutting staff numbers. The marginal labour decision would move from whether marginal revenue exceeded full wage cost to whether it exceeded immediate *cash* cost. This lower figure suggests that *more* marginal staff would be employed.

9   Trading losses that exceed a corporation's reserves will be borne by those who are both charged with the duty of the corporation's control and in a position to alter the direction of it. This will give confidence to suppliers, increase the incentives for a

corporation to continually re-invest, reduce equity holder anxiety for early cash returns in favour of long-term success, and focus the attention of those in control. It was concluded in Chapter 10 that this would not necessarily reduce the boldness of management decisions, but it would reduce recklessness and apathy – and would greatly enhance business confidence among suppliers.

10 By identifying the equity *precisely* with the corporation's 'value added', there will be a move away from the traditional targets of turnover, net profit, earnings per share and share price as the principal measures of corporate success, and the adoption instead of *value added* as the proper measure. Growth in value added brings *real* economic wealth: corporate success will be measured in precisely the same terms as most economists wish to see for the nation as a whole – economic growth, or putting more goods and services into more people's hands.

11 In some corporations there may be equity holders whose driving purpose is not simply economic growth or financial reward. The benefit of vesting the ownership and control of a corporation's equity in the hands of those most relevant to it, is that those persons can now give expression to individual motivations. The *power to decide* on the corporation's personality in society is then vested in those most likely to be affected and most able to implement it. (This contrasts sharply with the limitations of the present model, which requires an exclusively financial motivation and then even applies *this* through a somewhat remote process.)

It then becomes a genuine practicality for the current equity holders to freely decide what objective they presently want for their corporation. Economic growth, customer satisfaction, producing the finest quality products, providing the highest level of employment, keeping prices as low as possible... it is for the equity holders to decide, and this objective can vary with time. At present many corporations seem to strive for considerable uniformity and standardisation of products or services (for example, in rigid and centralised banker/customer relationships, in limited menu choice in fast food chains); these are ruthless efficiencies intended solely to increase shareholder value, but often have a greater cost in other directions which at present are out of view.

12 In established corporations, competent and enterprising directors and their supporting workforce would see a very substantial reward for their efforts in the medium to long term, and there should be less conflict between equity holders and directors in deciding what really is the principal mission of the business. Ineffective directors will be more readily apparent to the equity holders/governing committee, and more promptly dealt with. The structural authority of the governing committee should also help to control excessively dominant directors in a way in which mere non-executive directors or individual shareholders could never do.

The community at large is likely to see the benefit of more care and quality built into the management and operation of corporations (because of the deeper involvement of those within the company), more consistency (because of the greater solidity and independence of corporations) and yet at the same time more variety (because of their independence and probable smaller size). Customers in particular may well have more regard paid to their interests as suggested in paragraph (1) above in this list.

Competitiveness should be improved: while the workforce should enjoy more of the fruits of their labour, this is not the same thing as increasing their wages. Indeed wages themselves may even go down, while the employees' share of profits should rise; and as this profit is taken from the same source as is available to the existing capital providers, that does not push up prices, and therefore does not create problems in competing with imported goods and services. The incentive is, in fact, to keep prices down so as to increase long-term profits by securing the market niche. With no minimum rates of dividend to pay out, it should be easier for an established company to survive on leaner margins in difficult times. Finally, the clearer identification of the directors and the workforce with the success of the corporation should give those actually operating the business more 'proprietorial' control of the corporation and a greater incentive for efficiency. The whole ethos should become one of greater care and concern – of unity and harmony – with a reduction in frivolous waste.

13 The rigid framework of the steam-driven Victorian corporation would finally disappear, and be replaced by a more dynamic and flexible model that adjusts fully to market demands and external circumstances, and reflects a much more contemporary cultural outlook.

...to the end
Perhaps we should now return to the concept of 'self-organisation', which was the starting point of this book, and imagine a corporation with an independent, organic nature. Able to respond and adapt to all sorts of unforeseen changes in circumstances; powerfully independent, yet closely supervised by, and answerable to, all those most committed to and involved in it; directors able to offer equity for short, critical but limited periods to those whose contribution to the company (whatever form it takes) is most needed at the time; directors, senior management and the entire core workforce able to freely and legitimately enjoy the financial fruits of success without having to pretend to be shareholders; a body of strategic participators prepared, in hard times, to forego immediate full payment for their goods or services, including even a reduction in wages, in return for sharing the subsequent equity: a flexible 'live' organism, with its constituent parts all working together, instead of a rigid, mechanical structure with a confrontational constitution.

The implications for economic and financial policy makers extend far beyond the mere modernisation of the present corporate model. The impact would not only resolve the structural flaws which are of increasing concern in the present model, but would also lead to profound changes in the very dynamics of business enterprise: the real prospect of a working relationship between the different parties contributing to corporate economic activity; a freeing of valuable risk capital for recycling to other new businesses; structural motivation for directors and all those materially relevant to the creation of wealth; and a transformation from the present malaise of short-termism. Over the longer term, corporations will tend to accumulate greater resources, so that a greater share of equity might pass from the 'outsiders' (the heirs to those who originally helped to set it up), to those within the corporation who now have the task of keeping it all going. Capital will have been made available to enterprise and labour, in return for profit; but in time this will enable enterprise and labour to create their own capital resources, within their own corporation and under their own control: an automatic redistribution of wealth, but only to those actually generating it, and away from those simply leaving it idle. This, together with the other motivations identified in this book, should lead to genuine, sustained economic growth.

14 Conclusions

Elsewhere in this book, we commented on how marvellous the present situation of modern man might be. The irony is that, while we may increase material prosperity, and even individual freedom and advancement and so on, this does not equate with *contentment*. Perhaps it is that dissatisfaction with the existing state of things seems to be built into the human psyche, thus ensuring constant progress. But there is something more specific than that: market economics is founded on the concept of *competition*, and there is an inherent, irreconcilable conflict between competition and co-operation. It is intrinsic in the concept of competition that there will be winners and losers. The very flexibility we seek for increasing employment, for example, increases inequality in economic returns. This competition is of course the very spur of the free market system, but it is also the cause of much unhappiness, a sense of failure and inequity, a cause of greed and jealousy. Many modern commentators argue that there needs to be a greater sense of inclusiveness, a far broader range of winners. Ideally the system should be seen to be structured in a way that benefits as wide a range of participators as possible, and to do so automatically rather than by concession or necessary confrontation.

The ideal objective for economic activity is not really economic growth in total, on its own. It is surely the *maximum spread* of that economic growth. It seems false to suggest that there is overall success if this economic growth is concentrated in the hands of an elite, such as under the feudal system, or in the hands of the winners in a supremely individualistic society, such as modern Russia, Nigeria or the even the USA. The measure of economic success in a liberal democracy can only really be the maximum economic growth spread over the maximum number of people – a sort of 'utilitarian' version.

It is not being argued that there should be redistribution of wealth in order to achieve fairness, i.e., that wealth ought to be redistributed by command, taking from some to give to others, so as to be fairer. The issue is rather whether the arrangements for an economy can truly be said to be successful if they do not naturally and automatically achieve, as an outcome, a reasonably fair distribution of wealth as a matter of course, without intervention.

If the aim of civil and economic advancement is *not* to make life more comfortable, healthier, fairer and more enjoyable for as great a proportion of society as possible, then what *is* its aim, bearing in mind, of course, that this aim needs to have the support of the majority of the population in a liberal democracy?

One of the problems with the present corporate model is that participation in industry and commerce (i.e., the stuff of daily living for most people) is in danger of being reduced to a simple formula of financial greed. Economists have long described man as a rational being, but actually, if you think about it, they've got that quite wrong. It is not *reason* that drives mankind, it is his *instinct*. We do not apply logical reasoning to how we behave, we live according to our instinctive preferences. We warm particularly to those we identify with, and yet we also have empathy with those who suffer, even when we don't know them. We have a sense of justice and fairness that often trumps the urge to be selfishly greedy. And this error of economics *matters*, because it means that the economic models and the structures they support are flawed, and if they are flawed, then they simply don't work as they should.

Many individuals, for example, value culture and civilisation above pure salary, yet shareholders are simply not allowed to; the wholeness of the investor, as a human participant, is simply not recognised.

With capitalism there is often an atmosphere of remoteness, facelessness and fragmentation, the individual feeling powerless in the sense of the whole, and therefore turning increasingly to a selfish individuality. Often for workers and junior and middle management, the purpose and the substance of adjacent work areas is shrouded in unnecessary confidentiality – there is obsessive secrecy (i.e., exclusion) where openness would risk little and gain much. There is accordingly an absence of any sense of belonging, and little opportunity for the expression of non-economic self-worth, of culture and of altruism. Economic activity finds it difficult to accommodate this within its present structures. Yet if economics is to be the academic study of the major elements of human interactions, then it must accommodate it.

If value is not attributed in some way to what matters to people, then the economic systems can hardly be expected to work towards the best interests of human society. Without converting the rest of the picture into economic terms, economics is bound to be only part of that picture. This means that it does not adequately model the whole, and cannot therefore be expected to achieve what society asks of it.

Perhaps we should be encouraged to step back for a moment and consider thoughtfully what we really want for the future of society. Left on its own, untamed, the market economy can only express itself in monetary terms. This means that there are some matters – deemed important to society – which the market economy simply cannot deliver: defence, law and order, welfare and so on. We know all this, but there are other matters too, and we do not always think these through. For example, do we *really* want to lose all village general stores and post offices, and be left solely with huge town centre shopping malls and out-of-town supermarkets? Are we *really* right to lose local railway stations? Are we *really* right to let the capitalist free market drive us to homogenise the high street of every town and city, and standardise fashion and culture the world over, in the pursuit solely of shareholder returns? To provide fabulous, exclusive restaurants for the rich and standardised fast food outlets for the rest of us? Diversity and individual independence are often awkward and inefficient, just like diversity in agriculture, but they are ultimately far healthier for all of us than monoculture. Pure ruthless efficiency is hardly the stuff a contented, civilised society can be proud of. Indeed, it could be argued that social relationships (which represent the cultural quality of being civilised) are often more fully and deeply embedded in primitive civilisations than in modern urban ones.

When judgement on these issues is reduced solely to the limited factors of economics and viability at the time, society can be forced into changes in a way that it would not perhaps have chosen. The ultimate society for pure 'capitalist' free markets is probably not unlike the common image of apartheid South Africa – lines of mighty individual fortresses with private gyms and swimming pools for the successful, and a completely non-integrated shanty-town society for everyone else outside the gates.

It is probably a misreading of the nature of human society, ancient or modern, to presume that an activity which requires effort will not be undertaken unless there is an economic gain in prospect. On the contrary, much of what is of the greatest value to individuals and to the world as a whole – especially where this is not by popular demand – is undertaken at great effort or sacrifice and yet with little or no prospect of economic gain. Individual self-fulfilment in art and culture, amateur sportsmen, religious devotion, family commitments, the unpaid work of charity trustees, school governors, local councillors, the list is endless. Profit is but a single motive, and not necessarily the most potent.

It is possible to argue that many of the great milestones in the recent development of modern human civilisation were achieved *despite* rather than because of economic market pressure: the abolition of workhouses, the emancipation of servants and slaves, the curbing of exploitation and of sexual and racial prejudice, the introduction of a culture of fairness, equality before the law, justice, health and safety. (Legislation sometimes precedes public opinion, though unfortunately with economic structures and institutions it tends to follow slowly behind current thought.) The free market can become dangerously obsessive and one-dimensional, with its ingrained revulsion for regulation and the dependency culture in particular. The answer has so far been to try to strike a fair balance between the two extremes, but sometimes with adversarial consequences.

This book proposes above all else that the two concepts become more comfortably integrated. Civilisation is said to be the victory of reason (i.e., conscious rational thought) over pure instinct/nature: but the aim must be for both reason and instinct to be incorporated more effectively into human economics, to be built into our economic structures. We must be able to have – and to treasure – a stake in the task to which we devote our working life, without this being capable of being expressed solely in terms of monetary gain.

So what are we saying? That capitalist market economics, as presently structured, is not the great and all-inclusive success that it is often made out to be; but with a number of structural changes it *could* be dramatically improved.

The various structural changes proposed in this book are intended to achieve that improvement, and the philosophical drive behind them could be set out as follows:

- The broadening of the benefits of economic growth, by freeing the artificial bondage of equity to capital

- the structural recognition of drives other than pure financial greed, by introducing wider human choice into the control of corporate equity

- the valuing of limited resources for their own sake and not just for what profit man can make out of them, by actively and routinely pricing such natural resources

- the promotion of employment by making the creation of employment a success rather than a cost to be minimised, by adapting the economic test of commercial viability to encompass more marginal projects, by relieving or removing the burden of wages taxation, and by incorporating core employees into the company structure as participators

- the encouragement of business enterprise by putting directors at the heart of corporate activity, by rewarding all types of strategic contribution to business success, by reducing the cost of capital for successful companies (and spreading the rewards instead to the workforce), by reducing the risk of bad trading debts, by making value added (i.e., real economic growth) the principal target and measure of corporate success, and by identifying equity ownership with value added

- encouraging more new businesses of all sizes by enlivening the risk capital market through constant recycling of risk capital for investment

- giving the company a natural 'organic' flexibility to enable it to cope automatically with all sorts of different changes and challenges

- recognising that the cost of government is a cost to be met out of the creation of economic wealth, just as this is the source of support for everyone else. Tax is not a matter of taking from one individual to give to another, but something to be funded from the heart of the process of generation of wealth rather than after the point of distribution

- removing the vexed need for value judgement and adversarial pricing attaching to all non-capital participators in the corporation: directors and other strategic contributors to economic activity should be included in the free-market bargaining mechanism, just like capital is now, and be rewarded accordingly

- including within mainstream economic activity as great a proportion of the population as possible.

All of these changes are needed if mankind is to have a civilised and culturally rich society. The corporate model, the welfare system and the overall environment need to be brought into an integrated, more 'organic' economic system.

Finally we need to humanise the concept of 'ownership' if it is to be more appropriate to human society. A human life does not last forever, nothing does. In today's economic world, the arguably most valuable commodities – information and intellectual property – are surprisingly short-lived too. Yet certain artificial human constructs are declared to last forever, for example freehold ownership, hereditary titles, and shares in corporations. While the first of these probably still has much relevance in the market economy, with lasting occupation being valued, the latter two are quite incongruous and wholly incompatible with a modern, organically evolving and competitive market economy. The artificial permanence of share ownership and therefore the absolute permanence of ownership of productive capital have been disposed of in the new model of the corporation proposed in this book.

Economic activity is at the heart of civilised human life. It is the source of our comfort, security, nourishment, occupation and fulfilment. It is the source of the funding to help the least advantaged and to provide the overall management of society through government.

At the heart of this economic activity is the corporation, which is the framework within which most economic activity takes place. Like the rest of life and nature, this corporation needs to be organic, flexible and dynamically adaptable to the surrounding circumstances as they change. It needs to be able to take advantage of all the opportunities that arise, and to make the most of – and belong to – all the different contributors available to it. And it needs to be relevant to all of us, sharing the benefits as fairly and equally as possible in a way that promotes its activities.

That is the broad aim for these new proposals, however flawed some of the finer details may turn out to be.

References

Page

14. Hobbes, Thomas. (1651), *Leviathan*

15. Plato. (c.400BC), *Republic*

65. The London Stock Exchange website, accessed 27.10.14: *http://www.londonstockexchange.com/exchange/prices-and-markets/stocks/indices/summary/summary-indices-constituents.html?index=UKX*

75. Lovelock, J.E. (1979), *Gaia, A new look at life on Earth*, Oxford: Oxford University Press

92. *The Economist Newspaper Ltd,* London, 12th March 1994

114. *The Economist Newspaper Ltd,* London, 13th December 2014

121. Mayfield, Sir C. (chairman of the John Lewis Partnership), *Economia*, November 2014

138. Hatherly, D. (2014), In it together, *Economia, 28,* pp 68-69

172. Murphy, L. and Nagle, T. (2005), *The Myth of Ownership*, paperback edition, Oxford: Oxford University Press.

174. Office for Budget Responsibility, *Economic and Fiscal Outlook,* March 2012

175. Smith, A. (1776), *An Inquiry into the Nature and Causes of the Wealth of Nations*

176. Nozick, R. (1974), *Anarchy, State, and Utopia,* Oxford: Blackwell

Made in the USA
Charleston, SC
24 August 2015